EMOTIONAL MARKETING: ANALYSIS OF CONSUMER BEHAVIOUR THROUGH SOCIAL MEDIA

The Case Study of Groupe Nordik

OAXIES® PUBLISHING SPA RESEARCH SERIES

Simone Esposito, MSc, BSc (Hons)

EMOTIONAL MARKETING: ANALYSIS OF

CONSUMER BEHAVIOUR THROUGH SOCIAL MEDIA

The Case Study of Groupe Nordik

OAXIES® PUBLISHING SPA RESEARCH SERIES

Simone Esposito, MSc, BSc (Hons) | s.esposito@oaxies.com

EMOTIONAL MARKETING: ANALYSIS OF
CONSUMER BEHAVIOUR THROUGH SOCIAL MEDIA
The Case Study of Groupe Nordik

Published by OAXIES® LTD
Roseneath, 4 Hardwick Mount, Buxton SK17 6PP, UK
http://www.oaxies.com | info@oaxies.com

OAXIES® LTD is a company registered in England and Wales
Company Number: 10233754

OAXIES® is a trademark registered in the EU
Trademark Number: 016025595

ISBN-13: 978-1-9998205-3-4
ISBN-10: 1999820533

1st Edition, Copyright © 2019 by OAXIES® LTD

All rights reserved. The text of this publication, or any part thereof, many not be reproduced or transmitted in any form or by any means, electronic or mechanical, including photocopying, recording, storage in an retrieval system, or otherwise, without prior permission of the publisher.

All trademarks used herein are the property of their respective owners. The use of trademarks or brand names in this text does not imply any affiliation with or endorsement of this book by such owners.

Copy Editing by Ilaria Poluzzi | i.poluzzi@oaxies.com
Cover Photo and Graphic Design by Simone Esposito | s.esposito@oaxies.com

Printed by CreateSpace, An Amazon.com Company

TABLE OF CONTENTS

AUTHOR 9
    Simone Esposito, MSc, BSc (Hons) 9
ACKNOWLEDGMENTS 11
ABSTRACT 13
LIST OF TABLES 17
1 INTRODUCTION 19
2 LITERATURE REVIEW 23
    2.1 INTRODUCTION 23
    2.2 THE SPA INDUSTRY 23
    2.3 EMOTIONS 26
    2.4 EMOTIONAL MARKETING 30
    2.5 SOCIAL MEDIA MARKETING AND E-CRM 33
    2.6 SOCIAL MEDIA 35
        2.6.1 FACEBOOK 37
    2.7 CONCLUSION 39
3 RESEARCH METHODOLOGY 41
    3.1 INTRODUCTION 41
    3.2 AIM AND OBJECTIVES 41
    3.3 THE COMPANY BACKGROUND, GROUPE NORDIK 42
    3.4 RESEARCH PHILOSOPHY AND ORIENTATION 44
    3.5 RESEARCH APPROACH 45
    3.6 RESEARCH DESIGN 46
    3.7 RESEARCH METHOD 47
    3.8 SALMPLING TECHNIQUES AND LINES OF ENQUIRY 50
    3.9 METHODS OF DATA ANALYSIS 50
    3.10 VERIFICATION CRITERIA 55
    3.11 ETHICAL CONSIDERATIONS 57
    3.12 CONCLUSION 59
4 ANALYSIS AND DISCUSSION 61

4.1 INTRODUCTION 61
4.2 DISCOURSE ANALYSIS 61
    4.2.1 WINTER AT NORDIK 61
    4.2.2 MASSANA NATURE IN THE WINTER 68
    4.2.3 WINTER AT THERMEA 73
    4.2.4 KALLA TREATMENT 80
4.3 DISCUSSION 84
5 CONCLUSIONS AND RECOMMENDATIONS 89
BIBLIOGRAPHY 93

AUTHOR

Simone Esposito, MSc, BSc (Hons)

After the BSc (Hons) International Spa Management at the University of Derby, he is currently achieving the homonymous MSc.

Beauty Therapist, specialised in massage and spa treatments, has worked in Italy and England covering different roles in the Beauty & Spa Industry.

With Ilaria Poluzzi he has founded the brand Oaxies®, a start-up company specialised in spa maagement, with headquarter based in Buxton, UK.

ACKNOWLEDGMENTS

I would like to thank you and express my gratitude to Dr Iride Azara, my partner Ilaria, my daughter Sally Sophie, my parents Graziella and Giuseppe, my grandmother Eva and my uncle Edgardo.

GRAZIE!

ABSTRACT

The spa and wellness industry is increasingly expanding in most of the world (Lagrosen & Grundén, 2014), but despite that (Buxton, 2018; Global Wellness Institute, 2014; Tabacchi, 2010), there is still very little research done in this area, almost neglected by researchers and largely unexplored (Lagrosen & Grundén, 2014).
Several authors have requested further studies (Guillet & Kucukusta, 2016; Buxton, 2018; Loureiro et al., 2013; Reitsamer, 2015) as an opportunity to investigate factors that contribute to the formation of memorable experiences (Pine & Gilmore, 1998) and many have written about how to involve the customer in order to get this experience, with managers offering unique and multi-sensory experiences to create value (Berry et al., 2002).

Recent studies have shown how purchasing choices and decisions are the result of a careful analysis of both rational and emotional aspects, since emotions play a key role in any kind of social or business decision (Cislaghi, 2011). A good marketing strategy identifies how to give the opportunity to live a memorable experience (Ferrari, 2016, 2009, 2005; Pine & Gilmore, 1999). These results are of obvious importance for marketing and communication studies, as it can be an effective mean of pushing to purchase, to be implemented by strong brands, exploiting their benefits in terms of performance, to achieve an emotional agreement with consumers (Ferrari, 2016).

Given the rapid development of social media and web 2.0, changing people's habits and the conditions for marketing (Lagrosen & Grundén, 2014; Ruane & Wallace, 2013), wellness and spa companies should use social media to create profitable interactions with customers. Those interactions could create competitive advantages over their services as, the value determined by this interaction, can help develop propositions of value, more oriented to their customer's desires (Lagrosen & Grundén, 2014). In fact, previous research has highlighted the value of these interactions, in order to create meaningful relationships with customers. Spas have a vast knowledge on how to create pleasant and healthy experiences, being the basis of their services, and sharing them on social media should be on a large scale (Lagrosen & Grundén, 2014).

For this reason, the aim of this study is to bring to academia and investigate whether emotional marketing through the use of social media can influence consumer behaviour, in the wellness and spa sector.
This, evaluating the efficacy of the Canadian Groupe Nordik's communication strategy, analysing comments of four emotional advertisement videos, posted on the Facebook accounts of the company.
In doing so, the research questions that have been set for this analysis are:
• Can brands transmit emotions and convey them correctly through the use of social media?
• Which is their impact on consumers?
• Are social media involving consumers' senses influencing their choice and behaviour?

The most appropriate choice was considered a qualitative research, following an inductive approach, in the form of a case study. It was then decided to develop a discourse analysis of comments, regarding four promotional emotional videos, chosen on the basis of certain criteria such as: the emotional impact given; the relevance for the study; the high number of comments, opinions and "Likes", representing discussions and debates; and therefore the discrete wealth of discourse (Calder, 1977).
The author deployed Netnography, or Internet ethnography, a qualitative marketing research method, adapted to study online

consumers' communities (Kozinets, 2002). The four videos were analysed individually, using the analytical structure and the key lines that emerged from the literature. The key results were then recombined, identifying the common themes which have been discussed, reflecting on those specific to each one.

The analysis has shown that emotional marketing, through the use of social media, can influence consumer behaviour since the four videos revealed theirselves as an efficient and successful marketing strategy: consumers expressed both their appreciation toward the ads, the brand and the places, manifesting their impatience to visit and experience a day at the spa, as the vision of the emotional videos has stimulated an interest in them. Or they expressed a desire to return, due to the good memories of the good experience had at the place. This can be seen as the main theme emerged, common to all videos. Moreover, viewers are not bored by watching emotional advertisements and the main reason for that, detected by the discourse analysis, is a feeling of involvement and engagement, confirming that if videos do not provide emotions, users are not engaged with them. Confirming previous research (Lagrosen & Grundén, 2014), findings have also shown and highlighted the value of interaction on social media, in order to create meaningful relationships with customers. However, other viewers expressed their aversion toward the ads and the brands, whose motivations is the brand position, seen as controversial and no longer comparable to their mission.

LIST OF TABLES

TAB. 1: Verification Criteria 56
TAB. 2: Ethical Considerations 58
TAB. 3: Emerged Themes 84

1 INTRODUCTION

The World Wide Web and mobile platforms have given the possibility to communicate using emotional expressions through social media, thanks to the use of graphic interfaces or different representations of emotions such as emoticons, emojis, texts, images, voice-threads, videos and video blogs. Nowadays we can publish instantly the expression of emotions (Tettegah, 2016).

However, little literature has been written regarding the relationship between emotions, psychology and use of technology; although some, in sociology and communication, have addressed this emerging topic of expressing emotions socially and the various forms of technology crossing them (interface or computer-mediated communication) (Tettegah, 2016, Bensky & Fisher, 2014; Kappas & Kramer, 2011; Karatzogianni & Kuntsman, 2012).

Despite the growth in the thermal sector (Buxton, 2018; Global Wellness Institute, 2014; Tabacchi, 2010), with the spa and wellness industry increasingly expanding in most of the world (Lagrosen & Grundén, 2014), there is still very little research done in this area, important for the people's well-being (Lagrosen & Grundén, 2014). A large amount of research has been conducted on traditional and recreational health care, but the spa and wellness industry is almost neglected by researchers, with its concepts practically unknown (Lagrosen & Grundén, 2014), reason why several authors have requested additional studies (Guillet & Kucukusta, 2016; Buxton, 2018; Loureiro, Almieda, & Rita, 2013; Reitsamer, 2015).

For this reason, this study wants to analyse the use of social media marketing in the wellness and spa sector.

In particular, the aim of this study is to bring to academia and expand the body of knowledge on expressing emotions through the use of social media, in the wellness and spa sector, from the perspective of the brand, investigating whether emotional marketing through the use of social media can influence consumer behaviour.

The author has decided to analyse the online comments of four emotional videos, posted on the Facebook accounts of the Canadian company Groupe Nordik, that operates in the spa sector, which has been chosen as case study.

In doing so, the research questions that have been set for this analysis are:
• Can brands transmit emotions and convey them correctly through the use of social
  media?
• Which is their impact on consumers?
• Are social media involving consumers' senses influencing their choice and behaviour?

In chapter 2 the author presents a critical review of relevant literature studies regarding social media marketing, in the spa and wellness sector, as an effective tool of expressing emotions from the perspective of the brand, investigating their influence on consumer behaviour. This chapter aims to be an initial discussion on the issues to be addressed and then investigated.

In chapter 3 the author explains the methodology chosen, which is a qualitative study with an inductive approach in the form of a case study, selected as the most appropriate one. A discourse analysis has been deployed on the comments of the four videos, all providing emotional impact and chosen because of certain criteria: relevance to the study, high number of comments, views and likes, representing discussion and debate, discreet richness of discourse (Calder, 1977). The research method deployed is Netnography, or Internet ethnography, which is a qualitative marketing research to study online consumers' communities.

Chapter 4 presents the results of this study, with the opinions of the spectators regarding emotional videos, whose themes resulting from the analysis are then discussed in relation to the relevant literature. Finally, chapter 5 forwards the conclusion and recommendations.

2 LITERATURE REVIEW

2.1 INTRODUCTION

This chapter presents a critical review of relevant literature studies, regarding social media marketing, in the wellness and spa sector, as an effective tool to express emotions, from the perspective of the brand, investigating their influence on consumer behaviour.

The aim is to be an initial discussion on the issues to be addressed and then investigated.

2.2 THE SPA INDUSTRY

The spa and wellness industry is increasingly expanding around the world (Lagrosen & Grundén, 2014), but despite that (Buxton, 2018; Global Wellness Institute, 2014; Tabacchi, 2010), very little research has been done in this area (Lagrosen & Grundén, 2014). A large amount of research has been conducted on traditional and recreational health care in the form of spas, fitness centres, masseurs, etc. but the industry is almost neglected by researchers within its concepts largely unexplored (Lagrosen & Grundén, 2014). Many have requested additional studies (Guillet & Kucukusta, 2016; Buxton, 2018; Loureiro, Almieda, & Rita, 2013; Reitsamer, 2015) in order to investigate which factors can contribute to the creation of memorable experiences (Pine & Gilmore, 1998).

As a matter of fact, Pine and Gilmore (1999) state that nowadays, customers demand new and memorable experiences, since the mere offer of services, mainly non-material, is no longer sufficient (Nilsen, 2015; Bærenholdt & Sundbo 2007): organisations have a duty to give clients experiences the satisfy them (Lo & Wu, 2014; Jang & Namkung, 2009; Berry et al., 2002; Babin et al., 1998) and to gain experiences and memories. In order to comply with their expectations, companies must organise a series of memorable personal events that they can enjoy (Buxton, 2018; Bharwani and Jahari, 2013) and engage in a personal way (Pine & Gilmore, 1999). In fact, the spas sell mainly experiences being themselves personal experiences for customers (Lo, Wu and Tsai, 2015; Ely, 2008; Remedios, 2008; McNeil & Ragins, 2005; Monteson & Singer, 2004), since we go there for a sense of well-being or for a multidimensional environment state, which includes the five senses (Wuttke and Cohen, 2008; Corbin and Pangrazi, 2001).

The word experience, introduced by Holbrook and Hirschman (1982), is one of the key elements to understand consumer behaviour. It is a subjective, personal, psychological activity, usually with an important emotional significance and based on which there is interaction with the products or services consumed. An experience can be activated by anything related to entertainment and sensory stimulation (Holbrook, 1999). Attention is therefore focused on the hedonistic characteristic of consumption, of fantasies, feelings and amusement of consumers, whose sensation of pleasure is given by the fun deriving from consumption (Holbrook & Hirschman, 1982). Highly subjective and intangible elements are the basis of health, wellness and medical tourism services, which, during the consumption experience, are completely involving the guest physically, mentally, emotionally, socially and even spiritually (Buxton, 2018; Smith et al., 2016; 2014; Pine & Gilmore, 1998).

In the consumption process, especially in the service sector, the most important element is emotions (Lo & Wu, 2014; Jang & Namkung, 2009; Babin et al., 1998; Westbrook & Oliver, 1991). Indeed, an individual responding to a service has an emotional reaction, called "consumption emotion", which makes him satisfied (Lo, Wu, Tsai, 2015; Richins, 1997).

Good experiences must be memorable, competitive and provide emotions, which are the heart of consumer experience (Lo, Wu & Tsai, 2015; Carù and Cova, 2003; Pine & Gilmore, 1999). It follows the personalisation of the guests' experiences, giving rise to a "transformation" for which the economic offer of a company becomes the change of the individual, and thus the birth of the so-called "transformation economy" (Pine & Gilmore, 2011, p. 54). An experience, in fact, occurs when services are purposely used for the individuals engagement (Pine & Gilmore, 1999).

Many have written about customer involvement, in order to create value through lived experience and, in the field of leisure and tourism, this awareness has increased with managers, offering unique aspects and multi-sensory experiences (Berry et al., 2002) that are rich in sensations and created within the individual (Buxton, 2018; Pine & Gilmore, 1998), with guests becoming part of the service (Holbrook and Hirschman, 1982) physically, psychologically and also spiritually (Caffier, 2017). This is why are classified as "comfortable gains", exp3eriences where guests are increasingly involved in their creation (Smith et al., 2016).

Previous research has highlighted the value of interaction on social media, in order to create meaningful relationships with customers. Despite this, it seems that many do not fully exploit these possibilities, considering social media only a mere channel of communication instead of interaction, preferring a greater number of likes to a greater number of comments and therefore of interaction (Lagrosen & Grundén, 2014). The interaction on social media is actively created by contributions from consumers and producers, in which the customer is always a precious co-producer (Lagrosen & Grundén, 2014).

Spas have a vast knowledge on how to create pleasant and healthy experiences, being the basis of their services, and sharing them on social media should be on a large scale but this is not always possible given the need of an organisation supporting that (Lagrosen & Grundén, 2014).

Given the rapid development of social media and web 2.0,

which is changing people's habits, particularly in young people, and consequently the conditions for marketing (Lagrosen & Grundén, 2014; Ruane & Wallace, 2013) wellness and spa companies should use social media to create profitable interactions with customers. Those interactions could create competitive advantage over their services as, the value determined by this interaction, can help develop propositions of value more oriented to their customer's desires (Lagrosen & Grundén, 2014).

2.3 EMOTIONS

Marketing has changed enormously since the 20th century until today, gradually evolving at the same pace as social changes and consumer needs. In fact, contrary to its beginning, in the late nineties, experiential and emotional marketing was born (Ferrari, 2016, 2009, 2005; Holbrook & Hirschman, 1982), whose focus was not just the distribution of goods and sales but mainly on consumers, the experiential consumption aspects as a holistic experience, and therefore, on their emotions and feelings (Ferraresi & Schmitt, 2018; Schmitt, 1999).

It was theorised by Bernd Schmitt and has several characteristics (Ferraresi & Schmitt, 2018; Schmitt, 1999). Its strategy is to involve consumers in unique and memorable experiences (Ferrari, 2009; Pine & Gilmore, 1999), which provide sensory, emotional, cognitive, behavioural and relational values, replacing functional ones. This approach considers how products and the related communication can improve the consumer experience (Ferrari, 2005; 2016) by extending the product concept to an analysis of consumption in the socio-cultural context (Ferrari, 2009; Holbrook & Hirschman, 1982).

Consumers are directed both rationally and emotionally to make choice of consumption logically and rationally, often conducted by emotions and directed to fantasies, feelings and fun (Ferrari, 2016, 2009, 2005; Holbrook & Hirschman, 1982).

It is difficult to define emotions because they are a complex set of interactions that act on many levels of our perception, helping to give depth to experiences (Gallucci, 2014). Indeed, there is still a continuous lively debate on the nature and definition of emotions in psychology (Panger, 2017).

First of all, when we talk about emotions we refer to a particular condition or tone, in which a person is found at a certain moment in his life or to express a mood and declare the involving effect of something (Gallucci, 2014). The emotional dimension enters into discourses and thoughts, in relation to the temperament, to describe a lasting state, or the mood when one wants to describe a basic emotional tone of the person, or to feelings when intervening lasting and intensity emotional toning changes often moderate or, finally, to emotions in the strictest sense of the term if the changes in emotional tonality are sudden, transient and of generally significant intensity (Panger, 2017; Gallucci, 2014). In any case, emotions are activated as a reaction to specific stimuli or situations and manifest themselves as coordinated systems that include: evaluation of stimuli; physiological changes; behavioural responses; affective resonances; cognitive resonances. Another aspect concerns the physiological nature of emotions, with variations in the states of the body and the brain in relation to a stimulus, which can produce changes in the heart rate, blood pressure and rhythm of breathing (Panger, 2017; Gallucci, 2014).

Therefore, by slightly changing the point of view, we can define emotion as the chain of events that trigger between a trigger (input) and the execution of the behaviour elaborated as a response (output) (Gallucci, 2014).

The psychologist Robert Plutchik (1995), developed one of the first organic classifications of emotions, that would be eight primary, innate and universal, the combination of which can give rise to secondary or complex emotions. According to his classification, the eight basic emotions are divided into four couples: anger and fear, sadness and joy, surprise and the waiting, disgust and acceptance (Cislaghi, 2011; Plutchik, 1995).

The Plutchik (1995) structuralist classification has been the more successful one because it is based on a real model that well represents the observations of reality, thus resisting empirical verifications. The model is developed on three dimensions: polar extremes, intensity and similarity. Moving along the polar axis of a fundamental emotion towards the bottom we find labels that identify emotions similar to the fundamental one but characterised by a lower intensity, while on the opposite side we find that of greater intensity. The third and final dimension is the similarity therefore the closer the emotions are the more they resemble each other. Plutchik (1995) then states that mixing different emotions produces others. This explanation is certainly fascinating, but not very useful in the field of marketing since this classification risks proposing labels and descriptions of emotions dependent on unscientific variables (Gallucci, 2014).

On the other hand, in the functionalist perspective the rather dimensional nature of emotions is emphasised, namely their variability according to different degrees of intensity that can be placed in a continuum (Gallucci, 2014). Wilhem Wundt (1896) already supported the polarity character of emotions, their dimensional nature and their variability to be placed along the three axes of pleasantness-unpleasantness, excitement- calm, tension-relaxation. Indeed, in the most recent functionalist perspective, emotions are interpreted as a kind of socially shared and biologically predetermined scripts (Gallucci, 2014). In particular, in this traditional view, this set of basic emotions are a psychological, physiological and behavioural responses strictly linked to specific regularity of the evolutionary environment, expressed through specific experiences and characterised by distinctive facial or body expressions (Panger, 2017; Ekman, 1992; Ekman, 1999; Fredrickson, 2001; Sabini & Silver, 2005; Tracy, 2014). The emotions are then associated with specific trends of action or with repertoires of action-thought (Panger, 2017; Fredrickson, 2001). In summary, basic emotions represent specific and universal adaptations that have evolved to promote survival (Panger, 2017). This model considers emotions not as innate and universal, but as a representation and interpretation of situations that are strictly dependent on each individual based on their own experiences and their own history. Therefore they would be psychologically determined as well as, to a large extent, socially shared. Emotions can be positive or negative, constructive or destructive, pleasing or unpleasant depending on what causes them and the situations in which the person finds himself (Gallucci, 2014).

Alternative visions consider a wider variety of emotions, detaching the "sensation- experience" pair of emotions from other processes traditionally associated with them (Panger, 2017; Russell, 2003; Russell, 2009; Barrett, 2009; LeDoux, 2014), and then the answers expressed by people are no longer closely related to the threat or fear (Panger, 2017; LeDoux, 2014). Emotions without the need for an automatic, strictly coordinated response, allows the recognition of a greater variety of emotions and allows greater variation within them. According to this vision, there are therefore no emotions outside of cognition, helping us to interpret, respond and communicate sensations from inside and outside our body. Emotions are experienced when we interpret our internal state, linked to the surrounding environment, so then different cultures could detect and assign different meaning to different sensations (Panger, 2017; Barrett, 2009).

Emotions affect us from an early age and at the moment it is widely accepted that emotions regulate, influence and even organise our behaviour, influence cognitive thinking and arouse our desires (Gallucci, 2014). The human brain functions independently of our will by producing models that it then compares, chooses and pursues.

It has two ways of receiving and assimilating: the first, the basic one, is pre-logical because it does not split the literal notion from the abstract one; the second, more advanced, is able to separate them (Gallucci, 2014).

The pre-logical state is that which makes emulation easier, that is the possibility of transforming everyday objects into myths, and which, when it assimilates the figures, decides not to know, to renounce or to refuse the splitting between literal and abstract notions. Emotions have a significant impact on our perceptions and also on the experiences we experience every day in interaction with products or services, and can be decisive in choosing a brand. Emotional experience is certainly pervasive of human conduct and it is difficult to think that rational conduct in a decision or evaluation can be immune to it. It is therefore reductive and unjustified to believe that the rational decision requires the cancellation of the influence of emotions (Gallucci, 2014).

Emotions are distinguished in fundamental (or primary) and higher cognitive. The first are universal and innate, born spontaneously and last a few seconds at a time. There is no agreement among scholars on their number, but on most lists are included joy, suffering, anger, fear, surprise, disgust. Among the fundamental emotions, happiness and sadness are missing which, in the evaluation most shared by scholars, are terms better used to describe moods. The higher cognitive emotions are also universal, like the fundamental ones, but they are more influenced by the cultural environment in which they manifest themselves and are slower to develop and disappear. These are love, guilt, shame, embarrassment, pride, envy and jealousy. Most scholars believe that there are also non-fundamental emotions that would be a combination of the most basic ones (Gallucci, 2014).

2.4 EMOTIONAL MARKETING

Emotional marketing is a new concept within marketing, that concentrate on how to induce emotions in order to push people to purchase (Ferrari, 2016, 2009, 2005) which studies have recently shown to be the result of rational and emotional aspects. Literature in psychology has recognised that emotional conditions can be influential at every stage of the purchasing decision process and that emotions, expressed verbally, facially and textually, are the protagonists in any kind of social or business decision (Cislaghi, 2011).

Consumers do buy goods not only for the real functions but also to receive an emotional gratification (Ferrari, 2016, 2005).
The brands have moved their competitive challenge to satisfy their target, since the consumer is a sovereign to whom present

intriguing, fascinating and surprising products, in a perspective that implies intangible desires belonging to the sphere of emotions (Ferrari, 2009).

This implies immaterial desires belonging to the emotional sphere (Ferrari, 2009) from which emotional and multi-sensory marketing and communication are born, which offer consumers emotional benefits (Ferrari, 2016, 2005).

Furthermore, scientific validity has been given to the brain division between the rational and emotional hemisphere, which differ as way of thinking and operating, but are similar in complexity and processing capacity, since high-level cognitive processes involve complex mental operations, directly related to emotions and behaviour; so, following the logic, like rationality leads to a conclusion, emotion leads to action (Ferrari, 2016, 2005).

The reasons behind consumption are given to us by the psychology of purchase behaviour, that is, units with lower rational control often determine the purchase and therefore the sensory stimulation aims to provoke a response and a consequent impulse of the consumer (Ferrari, 2009).

These results are of considerable importance for marketing and communication, because consumers receiving emotions are more likely to purchase, as well as build or strengthen loyalty to the brand, thanks to the emotional impact that creates an emotional relationship (Ferrari, 2016 , 2005).

Emotional marketing is therefore a set of strategies whose aim is the deep engagement of the consumer, based on the immaterial hedonistic, recreational and symbolic needs of the individual (Ferrari, 2009).

For this reason strong brands, to establish a level of emotional complicity with consumers, which represents a positive and acceptable value system, exploit their advantages in terms of performance, reaching an emotional agreement and creating a relationship of profound loyalty (Kotler et al., 2017; Ferrari, 2016, 2005). The emotional response, however, depends on many factors, of which the most important is the authenticity of a brand

(Ferrari, 2009).

According to Saatchi & Saatchi CEO Kevin Roberts (2005), the same principles of emotional relationships between individuals must be the same for the one with the brand.

Furthermore, Roberts (2005) states that brands struggle to become Lovemarks (Ferrari, 2016, 2005): that require respect and love, deriving from the ability of a brand to obtain mystery, sensuality and intimacy (Kotler et al., 2017, Ferrari, 2016, 2005), or the objectives that serve for an emotional bond with the consumer (Kotler et al., 2017; Ferrari, 2016, 2005) to be cultivated continuously (Ferrari, 2009).

Hence the birth of experiential marketing, theorised by Bernd H. Schmitt a professor at Columbia University, which is a strategy whose purpose is to involve the client in unique and memorable experiences (Ferrari, 2016, 2005; Pine & Gilmore, 1999) that must exceed expectations and anticipate unconscious desires, satisfying them. Experiential marketing is therefore a marketing activity focused on creating a bond with customers (Ferraresi & Schmitt, 2018; Schmitt, 1999).

A good marketing strategy then identifies which experiences allow you to live a memorable one (Ferrari, 2009; Pine & Gilmore, 1999).

The experiences take place in response to stimuli created by pre-marketing actions or during and after the purchase, through online or offline activities, and given by products, packaging, communications, in-store interactions, sales reports, events and similar; involving the individual and resulting from observation or participation in real, fantastic or virtual events (Ferraresi & Schmitt, 2018).

Brand and emotion are closely linked and brand strategies should be about "sharing emotions" rather than market share (Gobé, 2003). The brand is a valuable asset and investing in it gives stability to the organisation, given the relationship with long-term customers (Gobé, 2003).

The relationship between companies and their audiences has

been changed by the arrival of the web, digital media and technological interfaces, which give the opportunity to affirm their long-neglected needs, relying on entrepreneurial choices and strategies, as well as interpreting needs. People can not only guide the choices of brands and companies but also participate actively (Maestri & Sassoon, 2017).

2.5 SOCIAL MEDIA MARKETING AND E-CRM

There has been a transformation in marketing and consumer behaviour, as well as the way companies market, given the use of the web by over 3 billion people globally (Chaffey & Ellis-Chadwick, 2019, 2016; Chaffey and Smith, 2017).

The Internet offers opportunities for interaction that offer companies the ideal place to create experiences for consumers. However, there are still companies that consider the website as a simple information tool and not as an opportunity for entertainment and customer relations, through experiential marketing strategies (Ferraresi & Schmitt, 2018; Boccia Artieri, 2004) Companies, to enter the new communicative dynamics, must know how to use the web channels and tools, in order to create interactions and strategic relationships, continuing to stay on the market (Ferraresi & Schmitt, 2018; Boccia Artieri, 2004).

But through the new digital media there is easy access to more information and to the development and maintenance of relationships, thanks to social networks, which are places of contemporary experience in which build sensory paths, both individual and collective: the "media world" where to live social relations (Ferraresi & Schmitt, 2018; Boccia Artieri, 2004).

Digital marketing is the application of digital and mobile technologies, supporting the achievement of marketing objectives: acquiring new customers, providing services to existing customers and developing customer relations through E-CRM (Electronic Customer Relationship Management) (Chaffey & Ellis- Chadwick, 2019, 2016; Chaffey and Smith, 2017). In fact, the social media, have not only revolutionised our social relationships in everyday life but have become increasingly popular as a marketing tool for managing customer relationships, influencing people's purchasing behaviour (Lagrosen & Grundén, 2014; Ruane and Wallace, 2013). Social media marketing is based on a multi-way interaction approach, in which the roles of sender and recipient are mixed (Lagrosen & Grundén, 2014; Scott, 2010) since social media can create a fusion of value, created for an entire network, which includes customers and companies (Lagrosen & Grundén, 2014; Lariviere et al., 2013).

The pull-marketing strategy is more efficient for the use of social media, ie the company uses social media to communicate information, knowledge, values and ethics related to the service or product, in order to entice the customer to interact (Lagrosen & Grundén, 2014). If the customer is interested in interacting, valuable information on interests and preferences is exchanged, within an informal process that could influence further customer relationships and marketing activities, making the product or service more attractive (Lagrosen & Grundén, 2014).

Social media marketing is part of digital marketing, whose purpose is to encourage communication with customers or the presence on social media, blogs and forums. To take full advantage of the benefits, it is important to give customers the opportunity to participate in conversations, which are related to products, promotions or customer services, this to get as much information as possible about customers and give them support (Chaffey & Ellis-Chadwick, 2019, 2016; Chaffey and Smith, 2017). Social media marketing is accepted by most users, as long as it is not exaggerated, unlike other forms of communication (Lagrosen & Grundén, 2014; Hansson et al., 2013). By combining the use of different social media it is also possible to reinforce its effects. Social media is also an economic alternative, given the low costs, but many companies are still uncertain about how to use them (Lagrosen & Grundén, 2014; Lagrosen and Josefsson, 2011).

Social media marketing must be used by professionals for communication strategy or in planning the online marketing campaign (Chaffey and Ellis-Chadwick, 2019; 2016) by advertising within them, to reach and interact with customers: the contents shared or forwarded help awareness and sometimes even guide the response (Chaffey & Ellis- Chadwick, 2019, 2016; Chaffey and Smith, 2017). The advances in information and communication technologies (ICT), with an increased connectivity and social media development have radically changed the consumers' attitudes, expectations and purchasing habits (Leung et al., 2013). The communication of thoughts, opinions and feelings to other people, whether they are known (friends, relatives) or strangers is more easy.

A recent study by Nielsen (Kapadia, 2016), revealed that in the American market 80% of respondents use word-of-mouth (WOM) from friends and relatives when buying, while 67% use information on social media or e-mail. Indeed, consumers use word of mouth to search for information, to select offers and post-experience, to give their opinion or advise other consumers (Buttle, 1998).

By sharing experiences in real time thanks to the internet and social media, content flows of the same user are created, with different characteristics: any type of content or opinion is communicated and shared (Alharbi, 2015) with the possibility of leaving evaluations, reviews, posts and comments online (Evans & Bratton, 2008). And recently, have been shown by studies the impact of these reviews towards the behaviour of consumer when purchasing, in particular during: the search for information, the purchase decision and the post-purchase phase, when information support the decision taken (Kotler et al., 2018; Ye et al., 2011; Gretzel and Yoo, 2008).

2.6 SOCIAL MEDIA

Social media gain popularity in 2000 and in 2005 social networks were so popular because of the facility to put information online (Golbeck, 2015) since it is possible to post anything: updates or posts, something that a user publishes, a content, often short snippets of text, about what a person has done, links to interesting content, photos or videos; comment or reply, a common type of social interaction; photos and videos; metadata: information on updates, comments, photos and social connections that make up social media data, which often include the date, time of the update, the location (Golbeck, 2015).

The types of social media are varied: social networks, forums, photo sharing, review sites, and more. On social networks users can create accounts and build connections between them, post status updates, photos and other content about their lives or what they find interesting online; website dedicated to photos and videos sharing have limitation on the amount of text (YouTube, Instagram); Microblogging, blog in which to publish text online without having to have technical knowledge, which resemble online diaries, whose fundamental characteristic is the limitation of the text (Twitter, Tumblr); Social bookmarking, to collect links to liked pages online and share them with friends, with annotations or captions to the links and then organize them into categories (Pinterest); Social Games, to play video games together with your friends in different places; Apps, which means "application", small programs that work alone or within other social media sites that have their social experiences (Golbeck, 2015).

Social media have two-way communication, in which companies must participate actively and honestly, to be reliable (Evans & Bratton, 2008) and treat customers as friends (Charlesworth, 2009), emotionally linked with a direct relationship. Brands are then offered the opportunity to develop brand loyalty, customer-brand relations and brand awareness (Shupletcova, 2017).

The process of participation in social networks is dynamic thanks to the emotional aspect, derived from the relation between new friends and acquaintances: the individual is always at the centre and everything revolves around him, so the activity carried on is continuous and are cultivated interests, sharing information and experiences, and thus expanding the network of contacts (Gallucci, 2011) by socialising (Kotler et al., 2018; Charlesworth, 2009). Therefore, according to Kotler et al. (2018), they can communicate the experience before it is consumed.

Furthermore, the information has become the power of the customer who can search for information on products and services, deciding in this way what to choose (Charlesworth, 2009) based on reviews, descriptions or on the reputation of the company by other customers (Charlesworth, 2009).

2.6.1 FACEBOOK

Facebook is one of the best known "social media" or social networking site, and one of the most used in the world, with a strong emphasis on creating connections with friends (Goldbeck, 2015) allowing people to connect and communicate with each other (Panger, 2017; Boyd & Ellison, 2007). Facebook was born in 2004 as a web directory for college and university, but opened its doors to the public at the end of 2006, and now has 1.86 billion monthly users (Panger, 2017; Backstrom, 2013)

Facebook is divided into the News Feed and Timeline sections which is displayed to users along with recent status updates, or "posts", of "friends" (Panger, 2017; Backstrom, 2013).

The first is the central service, displayed from users when they open Facebook along with a collection of all recent status updates, or "posts", and/or activities of "friends" (Panger, 2017; Goldbeck, 2015; Backstrom, 2013). The news feed can be ordered in reverse chronological order, thus seeing the most recent posts first but by default, however, Facebook highlights the most relevant posts (Goldbeck, 2015). Indeed, Facebook, prioritises content from friends and relatives, based in part on user behaviour, from friends and relatives (Panger, 2017; Backstrom, 2013). Content shared via posts can be text, photos, videos, links, or status updates about what they are doing or feeling, who they are and where they are. Users can then interact by choosing one of the six emotional reactions (like, love, haha, wow, sad and angry), leaving a comment or "sharing" the post (Panger, 2017; Backstrom, 2013).

Instead, in the timeline, all the posts that a user has made are contained. In addition to user updates, all other personal data is aggregated and accessible to users from the Timeline (Goldbeck, 2015).

However, Facebook offers a range of other important features, including messaging and support for groups and events (Panger, 2017), and it is also a place where people share links, play with friends, publish photos and videos, share their position and find trendy news (Goldbeck, 2015).
Indeed, it is possible to do many things on Facebook: creating a list of friends, finding someone you want to be friends with by sending them a friend request, which once approved by the recipient, will declare the two friends, resulting in the possibility of seeing each other's updates; status updates, that is, how users share information, which is usually text but can also contain links, photos, videos and location information, sometimes tagging friends by name; interaction between users with status updates via "like", "comments" and "share", commenting is a way in which people can have a discussion while the sharing option is the way they can be republished, it is also possible to like a "page", managed by companies, celebrities or other public entities, by simply clicking on the "like" button (Goldbeck, 2015).

There is a mutual connection with people who generally know each other even in real life, but it is also possible to follow public figures (Panger, 2017; Backstrom, 2013). In fact, Facebook focuses on personal relationships: this is why posts often inform friends and family about important moments in life but also news discussions (Panger, 2017; Backstrom, 2013). The information posted by users are shared with their friends, who will see a list of posts once they log in to the site (Goldbeck, 2015).
Users can also create and maintain personal profiles, which contain background and demographic data (Goldbeck, 2015), being able to also browse through those of other people connected to them, or "friends" (Panger, 2017; Backstrom, 2013). In the "Information" section of the user you will find basic information, including employment, education history, personal traits, relational status, lists of relatives, the organisations they belong to and the things they like or have liked. In the "Friends" section

the list of his friends (Goldbeck, 2015).

2.7 CONCLUSION

In conclusion, the critical review of the literature regarding the use of social media marketing, within the spa and wellness industry, as a way of expressing and convey emotions to customers, has highlighted some gaps in the industry.

Indeed, the spa and wellness industry is increasingly expanding in most of the world (Lagrosen & Grundén, 2014), but despite that (Buxton, 2018; Global Wellness Institute, 2014; Tabacchi, 2010), there is still very little research done in this area, almost neglected by researchers, and largely unexplored (Lagrosen & Grundén, 2014). Several authors have requested further studies (Guillet & Kucukusta, 2016; Buxton, 2018; Loureiro et al., 2013; Reitsamer, 2015) as an opportunity to investigate factors that contribute to the formation of memorable experiences (Pine & Gilmore, 1998) and many have written about how to involve the customer in order to get this experience, with managers offering unique and multi-sensory experiences to create value (Berry et al., 2002).

Recent studies have shown how emotions play a key role in any kind of social or business decision, in particular purchasing choices (Cislaghi, 2011). A good marketing strategy identifies how to give the opportunity to live a memorable experience (Ferrari, 2016, 2009, 2005; Pine & Gilmore, 1999). These results are of obvious importance for marketing and communication studies as it can be an effective means of pushing to buy, implemented by strong brands by exploiting their benefits in terms of performance, to achieve an emotional agreement with consumers (Ferrari, 2016).

Moreover, given the rapid development of social media and web 2.0, changing people's habits and the conditions for marketing (Lagrosen & Grundén, 2014; Ruane & Wallace, 2013) wellness and spa companies should use social media to create profitable interactions with customers. Those interactions could create competitive advantage over their services as, the value determined by this interaction, can help develop propositions of value more oriented to their customer's desires (Lagrosen & Grundén, 2014). In fact, previous research has highlighted the value of interaction on social media, in order to create meaningful relationships with customers. Spas have a vast knowledge on how to create pleasant and healthy experiences, being the basis of their services, and sharing them on social media should be on a large scale (Lagrosen & Grundén, 2014).

For this reason, the aim of this study is to bring to academia and investigate whether emotional marketing through the use of social media can influence consumer behaviour, in the wellness and spa sector. This, evaluating the efficacy of the Canadian Groupe Nordik's communication strategy, analysing comments of four emotional advertisement videos posted on the Facebook accounts of the company.

In doing so, the research questions that have been set for this analysis are:
• Can brands transmit emotions and convey them correctly through the use of social
media?
• Which is their impact on consumers?
• Are social media involving consumers' senses influencing their choice and behaviour?

3 RESEARCH METHODOLOGY

3.1 INTRODUCTION

In this section the author illustrates and clarifies the methodological choice, firstly going through the research philosophy and approach, then concentrating on the design and methods, to conclude with the data collection techniques and the analysis procedures, focusing as well on ethical considerations.

3.2 AIM AND OBJECTIVES

The World Wide Web and mobile platforms have given the possibility to communicate using emotional expressions through social media thanks to the use of graphic interfaces or different representations of emotions such as emoticons, emojis, texts, images, voice- threads, videos and video blogs. Nowadays we can publish instantly the expression of emotions (Tettegah, 2016).

However, little literature has been written regarding the intersection of emotions, psychology and use of technology; although some in sociology and communication have addressed this emerging topic of the social expression of emotions, and the study of the various forms of technology that cross emotions, interface and other forms of computer-mediated communication (Tettegah, 2016, Benski & Fisher, 2013; Kappas & Kramer, 2011; Karatzogianni & Kuntsman, 2012).

Despite the growth in the thermal sector (Buxton, 2018; Global Wellness Institute, 2014; Tabacchi, 2010), with the spa and wellness industry increasingly expanding in most of the world (Lagrosen & Grundén, 2014), there is still very little research done in this area, although the importance of this sector for people's well-being (Lagrosen & Grundén, 2014). A large amount of research has been conducted on traditional health care, recreational health care in the form of spas, fitness centres, masseurs, etc. but the spa and wellness industry is almost neglected by researchers and the concepts within it remain largely unexplored (Lagrosen & Grundén, 2014), reason why several authors have requested further studies (Guillet & Kucukusta, 2016; Buxton, 2018; Loureiro, Almieda, & Rita, 2013; Reitsamer, 2015).

For this reason, this study wants to analyse the use of social media marketing in the wellness and spa sector.

In particular, the aim is to expand the body of knowledge on expressing emotions through the use of social media, from the perspective of the brand, and investigate whether emotional marketing can be put in place with the use of social media, influencing the consumer behaviour.

This has been put in place analysing the online comments of 4 emotional videos posted on the Facebook accounts of the Canadian company Groupe Nordik, that operates in the spa sector, taken as a case study.

In doing so, the research questions that have been set for this analysis are:
• Can brands transmit emotions and convey them correctly through the use of social
media?
• Which is their impact on consumers?
• Are social media involving consumers' senses influencing their choice and behaviour?

3.3 THE COMPANY BACKGROUND, GROUPE NORDIK

In order to better understand the background and the reasons that led to the choice of the case study, a brief overview and description of the company has been provided below.

The Nordik Group is a company specialising in the development of spa in harmony with nature, located in the Ottawa-Gatineau region. The group's goal is to develop innovative relaxation experiences by offering massages, body treatments and treatments inspired by Scandinavian relaxation techniques. In fact, the group's mission is to improve guests' health and well-being by offering a stimulating and regenerating experience, with the benefits of thermo-therapy and massage therapy, in perfect harmony with nature (Nordik, 2019).

In fact, the group's main mission is "to improve guests' health and well-being and to make a difference in people's lives by offering a stimulating and regenerating experience, with the benefits of thermo-therapy and massage therapy, in perfect harmony with nature". Its vision instead is "to develop structures that offer unique, unforgettable and beneficial experiences to all guests, with unsurpassed courtesy and service known as The Nordik Way" (Nordik, 2019). Precisely, the Nordik Group facilities offer natural settings in wooded havens with easy access to urban areas, guests are surrounded by wood, stone, water and fire (Nordik, 2019).

Nordik Spa-Nature of Chelsea, located in Quebec on the edge of Gatineau Park, opened in 2005. It continued to innovate and evolve by introducing unique relaxation experiences and eventually became the largest spa in North America. In 2015 Thermëa of Nordik Spa-Nature, the only Nordic spa in the Canadian prairies, opened its doors in Winnipeg. Currently, a new building of a third Spa-Nature in Whitby, located just 35 minutes from downtown Toronto, is under construction Construction. The success of Nordik's spa brought the rise of this thriving company to the top of the wellness sector (Nordik, 2019).

Nordik Group is really active on social media platforms: indeed, in addition to the website, it has a Facebook profile and an Instagram profile for each structure, and one for the structure under construction as well.
The group is really active online, posting different contents regularly, such as photos, videos, engaging text or challenges as

well, which help them to be very strong in interactions and engaging with customers. The difference between Nordik Groupe and most of companies in the spa industry is that they do prefer to build good relationships with the clients, through a very well managed E-CRM, receiving lots of comments and feedback, instead of just reaching as many "Like" as they can.

3.4 RESEARCH PHILOSOPHY AND ORIENTATION

To respond to a given problem, a set of beliefs and hypotheses are used, linked to the development of knowledge in a sector, which is the research philosophy. For each phase various hypotheses are posed on human knowledge (epistemological hypotheses), on the realities encountered (ontological hypotheses) and on the extent and ways in which values influence the research process (axiological hypotheses) (Burrell and Morgan, 1979) which they model the way questions are interpreted, the methods used and finally the results (Crotty, 1998). This is to have a credible research philosophy and a coherent project that can support the methodological choice, the research strategy, the data collection techniques and the analysis procedures (Saunders, et al., 2015).

This is qualitatively oriented study based on the paradigm of Interpretativism, considered the most suitable one for a thorough investigation on consumers and behaviours. Interpretivism is a subjectivist philosophy, according to which human beings differ from physical phenomena in that they create meanings, which are studied to create new and richer understandings of organisational realities, focusing on lived experiences and cultural artifacts, trying to include in the research participants and their interpretations (Saunders, et al., 2015).

When we want to deepen a complex market phenomenon, highlighting the variables and the influences between them, qualitative research can be useful. While, quantitative research may limit individual freedom of expression (Kotler et al., 2017).

Usually, qualitative research is associated with an interpretative philosophy in which we try to give meaning to subjective and socially manifested meanings, on a study phenomenon, in which the researcher is in a natural research context, to establish trust, participation, access to meanings and a deeper understanding (Saunders, et al., 2015; Denzin and Lincoln 2011).

Interpretationism, which developed as a criticism of positivism from a subjectivist perspective, is based on the fact that humans create meanings, then studied by the interpreters (Saunders, et al., 2015; Crotty, 1998) not like physical phenomena since there are people who differ in cultural background, in different circumstances, times and meanings, who create and experience different social realities. Interpretativist researchers try to take this complexity into account by collecting significant data (Saunders, et al., 2015).

3.5 RESEARCH APPROACH

The author has decided to chose an inductive approach, due to the type of research, in order to to construct a theory or develop a theoretical perspective more productive than the existing one in literature (Saunders, et al., 2015; Yin 2014). This approach starts with the collection of data, to explore the phenomenon and generate a theory, in the form of a conceptual framework (Saunders, et al., 2015).

Indeed, the literature has evidenced a lack of research in the area of study and current practices in the industry show that there is a need to develop further the topics (Saunders, et al., 2015). Thus, being this an explorative enquiry, the adoption of such approach enables the author to investigate the issues in depth with an aim of generating a working theory that can be used for further studies since, in an inductive inference, the known premises are used to generate untested conclusions to generate and build a theory, generalising from the specific to the general, using then the data collection to explore a phenomenon, identify themes and patterns to create a conceptual framework (Saunders, et al., 2015). The study of a small sample of subjects is usually more appropriate in an inductive approach, working with qualitative data and collecting them using a variety of methods, in order to establish different views of phenomena (Saunders, et al., 2015).

3.6 RESEARCH DESIGN

The research design is the plan that helps to manage the ways in which to answer the questions, including the clear objectives that derive from them and guiding the collection and analysis of data, taking into consideration ethical issues and constraints (Saunders, et al ., 2015; Bryman, 2004).

In this case, the research design is a qualitative study in the form of a case study (Saunders et al, 2015) analysing the efficacy of the Canadian Groupe Nordik's communication and the relationships between their corporate identity, image, reputation and branding. A case study is a thorough investigation into a topic or phenomenon within a real context (Yin 2014) in order to understand its dynamics, or the interactions between the object of the case and its context (Eisenhardt 1989, Eisenhardt and Graebner, 2007). Comparing, in these cases the various emotional promotional videos, the external validity of the data is strengthened, making use of a triangulation of the cases with the collected data (Yin, 2014; Saunders et al., 2015; Denzin and Lincoln, 2013).

In particular, the author has analysed Facebook comments from 4 emotional video advertisements, posted between 2015 and July 2019, on two Facebook pages (Nordik Spa Nature Chelsea & Thermea Winnipeg) of the case study, the Canadian company "Groupe Nordik", that operates in the spa sector.

The videos selected for analysis were: Winter at Nordik; Massana Nature in the Winter; Winter at Thermea and Kalla Treatments.

As explained in the literature, this organisation has been purposely chosen as an example of good industry practice. Indeed, Nordik Group is really active online on social media platforms: in addition to the website, it has a Facebook profile and an Instagram profile for each structure, and one for the structure under construction as well. The group post different contents regularly, such as photos, videos, engaging text or challenges, which help them to be very strong in interactions and engaging with customers. The difference between Nordik Groupe and most of companies in the spa industry is that they do prefer to build good relationships with the clients, through a very well managed E-CRM, receiving lots of comments and feedback, instead of just reaching as many "Like" as they can.

The single case study is the best choice if, as in this case, the researcher wants to analyse a single thing or a single group (Gustafsson, 2017; Yin, 2003) being able to question old theoretical relationships and explore new ones, carrying out a more careful study than gives the opportunity to better understand the topic (Gustafsson, 2017; Dyer & Wilkins, 1991).

In particular, in this case the author has decided to create a single case study with embedded units or to explore the case with the ability to analyse the data within the analysis of the case, between the analysis of the case and to carry out a cross analysis. This gives the researcher the power to see the subunits located in a larger case (Gustafsson, 2017; Yin, 2003).

For a deeper understanding of the exploratory subject and a complete description of the existence of the phenomenon, the application of the single case study can be not only advantageous but also the best (Gustafsson, 2017).

3.7 RESEARCH METHOD

In marketing decisions, it is important to understand consumers and their environment, knowing the answers to the questions, knowing their past experiences, motivations, fears, reactions to the campaigns, their loyalty, their use of the media. This also applies to social media; however, changing the methods for collecting information (Tuten and Solomon, 2014).

Social media have indeed expanded their possibilities of expression and researchers can monitor everything on public social platforms, whose contents can be very useful in order to obtain information to be used in marketing (Tuten and Solomon, 2014). Marketing research, particularly on social media, is both secondary and primary. Secondary research uses information already collected and available for use, while primary research uses exploratory and qualitative methods. After data collection, the analysis is carried out on qualitative results (Tuten and Solomon, 2014).

For this reason, it was decided to use the Netnography, or Internet ethnography, whose name derives from "Internet" and "ethnography", a qualitative market research (Kozinets, et al., 2014; Kozinets, 2010), adapted to the study of online consumer communities, with contextualized data, allowing the collection and management of online data for analysis and interpretation, based mainly on the analysis of textual discourse (Kozinets, 2002). Netnography is a methodology that shares many of the characteristics of ethnography (Kozinets, et al., 2014; Gubrium and Holstein, 2014) of which it adapts the techniques by studying the information available online to analyse attitudes and behaviours (Tuten and Solomon, 2014). The approach is dynamic, allowing scholars to explore and explain rich, diverse and cultural worlds (Kozinets, et al., 2014;) as online discussions take a closer look at consumer behaviour (Kozinets, 2002).

Moreover, Kozinets (2002) argues that this type of analysis is faster, less intrusive and more natural, than traditional ethnography, as it can gather a large amount of data without revealing its presence (Kozinets, et al., 2014; Kozinets, 2010). Indeed, it has a naturalistic orientation and approaches cultural phenomena in their local contexts, providing windows on naturally occurring behaviours. In particular, social media offers many advantages: access to large amounts of archived data, which can provide an unprecedented amount of information on members, values and cultural structures (Kozinets, et al., 2014; Kozinets, 2010) . The output of a netnography can be descriptive as well as analytical and the method tends to generate rich, thick description through grounded interpretations (Kozinets, et al., 2014; Willig, 2014), thereby providing a detailed representation of the lived online experience of cultural members. The research process is based on three steps: the choice of a suitable website and an appropriate speech (Facebook comments); data collection; and finally analysis (Kozinets, 2002), in this case a discourse analysis.

Discourse analysis focuses on how social and psychological realities are constructed and mediated by language, focusing on its constructive and performative properties and on the effects of the choice of words. Discourse analysis includes a careful examination of speeches and texts to understand how they convey the objects and subjects they talk about, based on the fact that words, spoken or written, shape the sense of the world and the experience of it (Willig, 2014).

Discourse analysis deals with the understanding of discursive construction processes and their social consequences, the product of which is our social and experiential worlds. The approach to analysis adopted in this study aims to generate insights on how participants in the discourse draw on the available discursive resources, for the construction of their own experiences, and their action within a particular context. Therefore, the analytical method adopted is influenced by a Foucauldian approach to discourse analysis, as well as ideas taken from conversation analysis and ethnomethodology (Willig, 2014). The analysis of the data from a discursive point of view is therefore concentrated on the language. In fact, the purpose of a discursive analysis is to better understand how the use of language, ie the choice of words, the grammatical constructions and the various rhetorical strategies, is involved in the construction of particular versions of events, of the effects of discourse, of what it can do and, consequently, the interest is directed to the discourse itself rather than to people. Any text can constitute a suitable data for the analysis of discourse (Willig, 2014; Parker, 1992), which can therefore be conducted on "texts" in a broader sense (Willig, 2014; Reavey, 2011; Hall, 1997). Furthermore, Potter and Hepburn (2005) argue that the data should consist of natural conversations, rather than written narrative accounts or semi-structured interviews. The analytical research of the discourse focuses on the role of language in the construction of social and psychological phenomena, dealing with the effects of discourse rather than human experience as such (Willig, 2014).

The analysis of the discourse proceeds through the text line by line, focusing on the language and allowing to produce a particular type of reading of a text, putting in the foreground language's constructive and performative properties (Willig, 2014).

3.8 SALMPLING TECHNIQUES AND LINES OF ENQUIRY

This study adopted a purposive sampling technique, to collect rich and deep data (Saunders et al., 2009; Veal, 2011; Veal and Burton, 2014; Bryman, 2015).
Each of the 4 emotional video advertisements was chosen due to certain criteria: satisfactory richness of discourse; high number of views, comments, with discussions and debates; different type of comments; diverse set of opinions, with a wide range of "Like" and "Dislike" data from the video; representation of a different sector and demographic data (Kozinets et al. 2014; Kozinets, 2002; Calder, 1977).

The line of enquiry followed was based on the following questions:
• Can emotions be transmitted and conveyed correctly through the use of Social Media?
• Which is their impact on consumers?
• Are Social Media involving consumers' senses influencing their choices?

3.9 METHODS OF DATA ANALYSIS

The author has decided to deploys a content and discourse analysis because of the top of research.
Content analysis is the study of the content of communication, included in a message, in relation to meanings, contexts and intentions (Prasad, 2008) to analyse written, verbal or visual

communication messages (Elo & Kyngäs, 2008; Cole, 1988) allowing the researcher to categorise words, phrases and the like, which once classified share the same meaning (Elo & Kynga¨s, 2008; Cavanagh, 1997).

This is to have a concise but broad description of the phenomenon, with concepts or categories describing the phenomenon, which will then go on to build a model, a conceptual system, a map or conceptual categories (Elo & Kynga¨s, 2008; Kynga¨s & Vanhanen, 1999).

Netnography is a relatively new method and so far analysis techniques have been developed in relation to similar procedures in ethnography (Kozinets, et al., 2014).

In particular, the author has chosen to adopt discourse analysis, which is the study of social life through language analysis in its broadest sense, including face-to-face discourse, non-verbal interaction, images, symbols and documents. It investigate the meaning, both in conversation and in culture (Shaw & Bailey, 2009). It analyses the language, in the common sense in which most people use this term that is talking, communication, discourse (Johnstone, 2018). The general principles of the analysis of critical discourse can be summarised as follows (Titscher et al, 2000; Wodak 1996): it deals with social problems, not with the use of language or language in itself, but with the linguistic character of social and cultural processes and structures, consequently, it is essentially interdisciplinary (Titscher et al., 2000). Society and culture are dialectically related to discourse and shaped by discourse, and at the same time constitute it. Every single example of use of language reproduces or transforms society and culture, and it is necessary to analyse the texts to investigate their interpretation, reception and social effects. Discourses can be understood only in relation to their context. According to Wittgenstein (1984), the meaning of an expression is based on its use in a specific situation (Titscher et al., 2000). Discourses are not only integrated into a particular culture, ideology or history, but are also intertwined with other discourses (Titscher et al., 2000; Wodak, 1986). The analysis of discourse is interpretative and explanatory and critical analysis implies a systematic methodology, a relationship between the text and its social conditions, ideologies and power relations. Discourse is seen as a form of social behaviour (Titscher et al., 2000; Van Dijk, 1993, Fairclough, 1989; Wodak, 1989). Indeed, the critical analysis of the discourse does not analyse the texts but the discourses, which have a wider application than texts and refer to the whole process of social interaction, of which the text is only a part (Titscher et al., 2000; Fairclough 1989). Discourse, or the language used in speech and writing, is therefore a form of "social practice", which implies a dialectical relationship between a particular discursive event and the situation, the institutions and the social structures that frame it. The dialectical relationship is two-way, since the discursive event models and it is modelled by the situations, institutions and social structures (Titscher et al., 2000; Fairclough & Wodak, 1997). Discourses are always linked to those produced before, simultaneously and subsequently, which are understandable only taking into account the underlying conventions and rules, that are linked to their historical contexts. The analysis of the discourse is therefore the analysis of the relations between the use of language and social and cultural structures (Titscher et al., 2000; Fairclough, 1995).

The selection of the case study and the data was made following the guidelines suggested by Kozinets, et al. (2014). Specifically, the researcher must choose a field site to study the most "research question relevant"; who has a "higher traffic of postings"; larger numbers of discrete message posters; more detailed or descriptively rich data; and more interactions between members of the type required by the research question (Kozinets, 2002: 63).

Furthermore, in netnography there are three types of data that can be collected: archive data, elicited data and fieldnote data. In this case the archive data will be analysed, that include everything the researcher can collect from the Web and is not the product of his involvement in the creation or solicitation of data (Kozinets, et al., 2014). These types of data can be the "cultural baseline", which expresses the community's behaviour before the researcher's incursion into the social media environment, which will help the researcher to deepen his knowledge of the cultural context (Kozinets, et al., 2014; Kozinets, 2010). These so-called observational data can be difficult to find, but, once found, they have relatively easy access with a very low cost gathering (Kozinets, et al., 2014).

It should be remembered that even text, in text, image or video format, has a context. In fact, in addition to text analysis, it is also possible to observe the way in which a Web page and posts are formatted, for example a conversation between various users, or to analyse the images used by people to represent themselves, the way they are described , the various signs and signals and the interactions between them (Kozinets, et al., 2014).

There are many ways to record data online but there are two basic techniques: the first is to copy and paste the content of a post into a word processing software file like a Microsoft Word document; the second is to capture a screenshot of data using a program.

Furthermore, the archive data can be present in the form of text, in visual forms, via audio, through video (Kozinets, et al., 2014). In this case, the data has been copied and pasted onto a word document, to be analysed later.

In particular, the author has deployed a discourse analysis of the comments of four emotional video advertisements posted on the two Facebook pages of the case study, which have been chosen on the basis of certain criteria such as their relevance to the study, the high number of comments, views and likes, which represent discussion and debate, in addition to the discreet richness of discourse (Calder, 1977).

Given the target market and the geographic position of the case study, the comments are both in English and French and, in order to have an easier understanding, the author has decided to analyse all comments in both languages from 2015 until August 2019.

The four videos from the case study were treated independently and studied making use of the analytical framework and the key lines emerging from the literature.

The major emerged themes were then identified and the key results were then recombined, with the common themes identified discussed, with a reflection on those specific to each of them.

The qualitative data analysis method is the coding, or "open coding" (Corbin and Strauss, 2008) in which the researcher labels and classifies data, meanings at field level, and groups these categories into other abstract categories, with final objective to reach a theoretically relevant understanding of the phenomena of interest. Different types of data can be organized with the same codes (Kozinets, et al., 2014; Kozinets, 2002). The theory that emerges from the coding is tested whenever new data is collected and analyzed, being collected specifically for this purpose. Cross-checking is facilitated given the easier access to data, often in large quantities. Comparisons seek convergence and divergence between coded data and categories (Kozinets, et al., 2014; Kozinets, 2002). Specifically, the comments were carefully prepared, codified and interpreted, using an inductive approach through which the comments were linked to the expression of themes and categories, to understand the users judgments, perceptions and experiences (Minichiello et al., 1990). According to the methodology line outlined by Kozinets (2002), to investigate similarities and differences, the data belonging to each category were compared with other data and codified as belonging to the same category.

Furthermore, in order to facilitate the analysis and an easier understanding of the comments, the author has decided to analyse both English and French comments, due to the company's the target market and geographic position. Finally, according to the ethics of citation or quotation, since online pseudonyms are often referable to real names and also because people do care about their online reputation (Kozinets, 2002), these have been treated as real names (Langer and Beckamn, 2005) and, when necessary, the comments were reported as "FBU1" ie Facebook User 1.

3.10 VERIFICATION CRITERIA

Interpretations and explanations in discourse analysis must be understandable so how the way in which the results were achieved must be recognisable. Specifically, the validity of the results is not absolute and immutable, but always open to new contexts and information, which in some cases could change the results (Titscher et al., 2000; Fairclough, 1995). The results must also be of practical relevance, since dealing with social problems the usability of the results is in fact a preliminary condition (Titscher et al.", 2000; Fairclough, 1995).

Mainly, in netnography the analysis of qualitative data proceeds in a similar way to that of any other comparable type of qualitative data, given the sharing of the inductive and iterative aspects of ethnography. There are four important requirements that guide the researcher in conducting netnographic data analysis (Kozinets, et al., 2014; Kozinets, 2002).

The first fundamental principle of quality netnography is ethnographic siting, to be specific on the site, focusing on a limited number of posts or data, in order to acquire a profound cultural sense of what is happening, to then be extended (Kozinets, et al., 2014; Kozinets, 2002).

The second principle of rigorous netnographic analysis is to undertake a cultural analysis of community members, or the rule of ethnographic engaging (Kozinets, et al., 2014; Kozinets, 2002).

The third is ethnographic communication, in which communications are, at least initially, experimented, elaborated and understood exactly as the members of culture experience them, that is, in the format of real natural text without filters (Kozinets, et al., 2014; Kozinets, 2002).

Finally, it is recommended to allow the ethnographic timing, so that messages and posts are lived, read, interpreted and analysed in real time, as soon as they are available, rather than all at once (Kozinets, et al., 2014; Kozinets, 2002).

The measures adopted to address the threats characterising

the chosen methodology, are illustrated in the table below.

Criterion	Actions
Coherence	Each recognisably different interpretation is devoid of internal contradictions and presents a unified scheme.
Rigour	Recognition and adherence to the procedural standards of netnographic research by the text.
Groundedness	The theoretical presentation is supported by data, and the relations between data and theory are clear and convining.
Innovation	The constrcts, the ideas, the structures and the narrative form provide new and create ways to understand systems, structures, experiences or actions.
Resonance	Obtainment of a personalised and sensing connection with the cultural phenomenon.
Verisimilitude	Achieving a credible and realistic sense of cultural and community contact.
Reflexivity	The role of the researcher is recognised bu the text and is open to alternative interpretations.
Praxis	Inspiration and empowerment of a social action by the text.
Intermix	The representation takes into account the internconnection of the carious modealities of social interaction, online and offline, in the members' daily experiences as well as their representation.

Tab. 1: Verification Criteria

3.11 ETHICAL CONSIDERATIONS

For social media research, there are still no ethical guidelines as they are relatively new.

In the context of social networks if, by virtue of the place where it was published, a content is in effect public domain then it can be used by the researcher. In the context of social networks, if the content was published in a place actually in the public domain, it can be used by the researcher, evaluating whether the data contains sensitive information and adopting the necessary measures to respect the policies and protect the people involved. Data, analyses and results must be made anonymous before being disseminated or shared. Finally, it is important to take the necessary measures so that the behaviour of the researcher and the use of the data do not cause damage (Tuten & Solomon, 2014; Kozinets, 2002).

Ethics (Mertens, 2014) is a complex and difficult topic in netnographic exploration. Since social media fuses the public and the private, there is a need for methodological innovation on issues of risk and privacy. Although knowing the real name of a user and having access to more information on offline life can improve the perception of the credibility of netnography, this carries the same responsibility to protect the identities faced by all other social researchers.

For archived data, the researcher can consider Web content as published content (Kozinets, et al., 2014; Bruckman, 2006; Kozinets, 2002).

Although a Web user is responsible for the consequences of publicly posting information on the Internet, with an original name or pseudonym, republication or citation in an academic publication may have unexpected consequences for the individual and / or the community and therefore the netnographers they follow the ethnographic tradition of pseudonymisation, protecting the names of individuals, both legal and hypothesised (Kozinets, et al., 2014; Kozinets, 2002).

Many web users have invested a lot of effort in creating pseudonymous identities and netnographers should be careful to protect these identities by creating additional pseudonyms. However, the fact remains an ethical and non-legal issue, since the information is published publicly under that name (Kozinets, et al., 2014; Kozinets, 2002).

Informed Consent	No informed consent was required as no interactions or interventions occurred, but the researcher used spontaneous conversations, analysed archived messages and existing posts.
Covert or Deceptive Research	NA
Debriefing	NA
Withdrawal from investigation	NA
Protection of participants	No risk of any physical, psychological or emotional harm to participants.
Observational research	NA
Giving advice	NA
Research in public places	The resercher used existing documents and records gathered in the publicly avaibalble communication system venue on the Internet where any person is aware that these systems are, by definition, mechanism for archiving, trasmissiona nd retrival of comments.
Confidentiality / Data Protection	• Netnography uses cultural information that is not given specifically, in confidece, to the researcher; • Onine pseudonyms have been treated as real names as they are often traceable to real names; • Data have been stored securely, collecting only data relevant to the study undertaken.
Animal rights	NA
Environmental protection	NA

Tab. 2: Ethical Considerations

3.12 CONCLUSION

The author has decided to choose a qualitative oriented study with an inductive approach in the form of a case study. To do so, the author analyses comments from four video advertisements posted on the two Facebook pages of the case study, the Canadian company Groupe Nordik, which operates in the spa sector, all providing experiences with emotional impact. The research method deployed is Netnography, or Internet ethnography, an online qualitative marketing research, adapted to the study of online communities of consumers.

4 ANALYSIS AND DISCUSSION

4.1 INTRODUCTION

In this chapter the author distributes a discourse analysis of the comments of four emotional video advertisements posted on the two Facebook pages of the case study, chosen following certain criteria: their relevance to the study, the high number of comments, views and likes, representing discussion and debate, a discreet richness of discourse (Calder, 1977).

4.2 DISCOURSE ANALYSIS

The four videos from the case study were treated independently and studied making use of the analytical framework and the key lines emerging from the literature.

The key results were then recombined and the common themes identified were discussed, with a reflection on those specific to each of them.

4.2.1 WINTER AT NORDIK

This video was initially posted on the Nordik Spa-Nature / Chelsea Facebook account on the 23 February 2015 with the bilingual title "Découvrez l'hiver au Nordik Spa- Nature, le plus grand spa en Amérique du Nord! / Discover winter at Nordik Spa- Nature, the largest spa in North America!" Every post have a bilingual title and caption, English and French, due to their target market and geographic position. It was then reposted on the 13 January 2016 with the title "Le Nordik Spa-Nature en hiver: une expérience magique! Nordik Spa-Nature during winter:

a magical experience", again on the 16 December 2017 "Ferric. Magic. Nordik" and finally on the 16 January 2018 "L'hiver au Nordik / Winter at Nordik" with a caption saying : "The third Monday of January is known as the most depressing day of the year. That's why we've decided to boost your morale with this video showing only the purest spa wellness. The day is looking better already".

The total of comments are 189 comments with 678 likes, 79 loves, 5 wow, the majority of them between 2016 (92 comments) and 2017 (72 comments) which makes deduce an overall positive opinion about the ad.

Given the target market and geographic position all comments are both in English and French.
As said before, in order to have an easier understanding the author has decided to analyse all comments from 2015 until now, both English and French comments.
In doing so, we can identify some major thematic emerging from this ad.

Watching the emotional video the majority of users, the 70%, have expressed their desire and wish to visit the place, experiencing a day at the spa

"Faudrait bien y aller!! / It would be good to go there"

Or expressing the willingness to be there already

"I wish I was there"

Others ask and refer to friends or partners to set a date to go

FBU1: "FBU2 FBU3 on y va quand la??? / when do we go there?"

Or

FBU1: "Girls day soon please FBU2"

And

FBU1: "C'est quand qu'on y va FBU2? / When are we going?"

Or

FBU1: "FB2 can we go?"

Or, underlining their desire to go after having watched the video, which can be seen as a successful marketing strategy with the ad

FBU1: "FBU2......when we going? I can't take it anymore lol.....watching these postings is making me want to go soooooo bad lol!"

FBU2: "Soon...i feel your pain, its nasty out there today...... (...)"

Some other starting already to arrange a day

FBU1: "If we can't go this weekend we have to go one day... FBU2 FBU3"

Or

FBU1: "FBU2 regarde comment on serait biennn, je sais que c'est pas trop trop ton genre mais ce serait un tres beau cadeau de saint valentin qui arriveeee / look how good would it be. I know it's not too much your style but it would be a very nice gift of valentine who arrives"

FBU2: "Ca (pourrais) etre une idee / This (could) be an idea"

And

FBU1: "FBU2 let's go this February"

Others refer already to an experience to be lived

FBU1: "FBU2 FBU3 FBU4, à quand NOTRE expérience magique? / FBU2 FBU3

FBU4 When will it be our magical experience?"

FBU4: "ca donne le goût!! / This gives the taste !!"

FBU2: "Ça ferait tellement du bien / It would be so beautiful"

Or highlight the beauty of the place, which is the main reason for their desire to go

"De toute beauté pas eu encore la chance d'aller vous visiter <3 / Beautifully, not yet had the chance to visit <3"

Moreover, other users have expressed their impatience in going to the location

"Looking forward to Valentine's Day. Hopefully not as cold as last year."

And

"Can't wait!!"

Or looking forward to their upcoming visit in the evening

FBU1: "FBU2 can't wait :)"

FBU2: "Omg, so excited to try in the evening."

Some, pointing out the details of the place to friends, emphasise their beauty

4 ANALYSIS AND DISCUSSION

FBU1: "FBU2 My god wow ! Pis on iva le soir check comment c'est beau les lumiere pis toute / My god wow! And we go in the evening check how beautiful is the light and everything else."

It is interesting to note how this user has initially commented on his eagerness to go

FBU1: "FBU2 FBU3 FBU4 can't wait!!"

Another feeling manifested by users is nostalgia, missing the place and the experience itself

"Ça ferait tellement de bien!!! La visite de cette ete ma ravit! / It would be so good !!! The visit of this summer delighted me!"

Or

FBU1: "FBU2.....faudrait bien y retourner bientôt. J'envoie ça dans l'univers. / ..... would have to go back soon. I send that into the universe."

FBU2: "Oui ça serait super le fun ! / Yes it would be great fun!"

And

"We need to go back!"

Or writing in capital letters to emphasise it

FBU1: "FBU2 FBU3! Let's go back! ☺"

FBU2: "FBU4 I WANNA GO BACK!" FBU4: "it looks beautiful"

FBU2: "It is, so let's go today. Right now :)" FBU4: "yeah haha"

Others both expresses their nostalgia and their good memories regarding the place, suggesting to open a new spa closer to them, in order to have the chance to enjoy more experiences

"Oh how I love and miss this place. Nordik Spa, pleeeease come open a spa on Newfoundland's west coast! Gros Morne National Park would be the perfect spot for your next adventure. ;)"

Some users, watching the video, have just expressed their real appreciation toward the place

"C'est le paradis le Nordik! / Nordik is the paradise!"

And

"J'adore cette endroit - un hâvre de paix!! ...et si près de chez-moi en plus!! :) / I love this place - a haven of peace !! ... and so close to my home! :)"

Or

"Omg I love it"

And

"It's so gorgeous!"

Or

"Très beau!! / Beautiful!!"

It is also of considerable importance for analysis purposes to pay attention to some comments regarding the video directly, expressing their appreciation toward its editing and the video itself, taking advantage of underling the beauty of the place

"Beau montage!!! J☐ votre coin paradis! (...) / Beautiful editing !!! I love your paradise! (...)"

And

"Wow beau cadeau en ce nouvelle annee 2016 un beau montage video... MERCIIIIII / Wow beautiful gift in this new year 2016 a beautiful video editing... THANKSSSSSS"

Other highlighting the power of relaxation of the video

"Ahhh merci beau petit video j'ai bien aimer ca relaxe juste a regarder et écouter. / Ahhh thank you beautiful little video I really like it relaxes just to watch and listen."

Or

"Wow! Très beau montage! :) / Very nice editing! :)"

Some also having a discussion regarding that

FBU1: *"Beautiful video, I was hooked after my first and only visit, can't wait to go back"*

FBU2: *"Yep, interesting post this is really great, more on please"*

Another important theme that emerged from the analysis is pride, or pride towards a brand belonging to its own territory, with the willingness to share this feeling with everyone

"Wow! C'est sublime et c'est ici chez nous dans l'Outaouais, que de chance pas besoin de sortir de ma région pour un service de spa A++ Bravo et merci d'être là! Fierté! / Wow! It's sublime and it's here at home in the Outaouais, that luck do not need to leave my region for a spa service A ++ Bravo and thank you for being there! Pride!"

This pride is sometimes associated with tourism, that is the recommendation of the spa to friends and relatives as a touristic attraction in the territory

FBU1: "FBU2 and FBU3 interested in going during your visit to Ottawa!? It's one of our favourite spots!"

FBU2: "Looks wonderful"

Or people from different areas seeing that as a landmark

FBU1: "FBU2 a must do for when we'll be in Ottawa".

4.2.2 MASSANA NATURE IN THE WINTER

This video was posted on the Nordik Spa-Nature / Chelsea Facebook account on the 22 February 2017 with a bilingual title "Massana-nature en hiver | Massana-nature in the winter" and the caption "Une expérience tout simplement unique. Il faut le vivre pour le croire. A simply unique experience available to you. You must live it to believe it".

It was then published again in the same Facebook page on the 10 January 2018 with the same title but a different caption "Massana-Nature, une expérience de détente unique au cœur du paysage hivernal! | Massana-Nature, a unique relaxation experience in the heart of the winter landscape!".

The total of comments are 157 comments (66 in 2017 and 91 in 2018) with 397 likes, 93 loves, 7 wow, which makes deduce an overall positive opinion about the ad.

As said before, the author has decided to analyse all comments from 2015 until 2019, both in English and French, highlighting the following emerged themes.
As for the previous video, most of the users, have expressed their impatience for their upcoming visit to at the spa

"J'ai hâte! / I'm looking forward!"

And

"Très hâte de l'essayer! :) / I can't wait to try it!" Or

"One week!"

And

"Wow very nice can't wait."

Or discussing with friends

FBU1: *"Can't wait!"*

FBU2: *"Me either!"*

FBU1: *"FBU2 this is what you have to look forward to on my birthday weekend!!! Xo"*

Again they have expressed their desire and wish to go visit the place, planning with friends, relatives and partners for a date

FBU1 FBU2: *"Je veux faire çaaaa / I want to do that"* FBU2: *"Moi aussi please / Me too please"*

Or

FBU1: *"FBU2 when are we going?!?!?!?!*

FBU2: *"Tomorrow? Lol just kidding. February some time"*

And

FBU1: *"FBU2 on devrait y aller bientôt / we should go soon"*

Other expressing the beauty of some details

FBU1: *"FBU2 on devrait y aller bientôt / we should go soon"*

FBU2: *"C'est beau aussi en soiree avec les lumieres et les bains / It's beautiful in the evening too with lights and baths ;-)"*

Other seeing the place the right location for an anniversary date or for saint valentine day

FBU1: *"FBU2 anniversary?"*

And

FBU1: *"FBU2 autour de la St Valentin on y va xx / around Valentine's Day we go xx"*

Or

FBU1: *"FBU2 for the 40's getaway???"*

Once more, users have expressed their desire to return

FBU1: *"FBU2 Quand est-ce qu'on y retourne? / When are we going back? ;)"*

FBU2: *"N'importe quand! / Anytime!"*

Or

"Seriously can't wait to go back!!!!"

And

"Let's go back"

Or

"We need to experience this again..."

Again people are sharing their memories regarding the good experience had at the spa

"Great Experience!"

In particular, one guest shared all the details of the stay, recommending the spa to other users and, in this case, the Nordik Spa Nature Facebook account in Chelsea responded to thank her for sharing the experience and inviting her for another visit, which can be seen as a successful engagement with digital users

"It was amazing! I'm from the UK and went with my daughter who lives in Ottawa in February 2016, on one of their coldest days, so I am not at all used to such cold weather. You can hire a towelling robe, or take your own, wear a hat, and wear flip flops, so you can walk between the pools and saunas. I felt wonderful afterwards and slept like a baby. No ill effects at all. In fact hot/ cold has wonderful health benefits (not that I can say I do this) (...) Go and enjoy a great experience."
Nordik Spa-Nature / Chelsea *"Good morning Carol ! Thank you for sharing your comments with us. We are very happy that your daughter and yourself enjoyed your spa day during your visit in Canada! We hope to see you again soon!"*

Once again the users have expressed appreciation toward the place

"Thebest!."

And

"Super de belle endroit , j'ai bien aimer çà ! / Super beautiful place, I love it!"

Or

"Love this place"

Or

"C'est tellement un bel endroit / It's such a beautiful place"

And

"Oui! Le lieu est magnifique (...)! On a le goût d'y être! / The place is beautiful (...)! We have the taste to be there!"

Advising to visit it many times

"Une place à visitez 2 fois par année minimum / A place to visit 2 times a year minimum"

Or suggesting a trip

"Next trip"

And appreciation toward the video as well, that stimulated an interest in going at the spa

"Magnifique à couper le souffle!! J'envisage venir pour une visite très bientôt / Beautiful breathtaking !! I am planning to come for a visit very soon"

However, for some users watching the video reminds of bad experiences at the spa, putting it in a bad light and in contrast with their mission, which is translated into aversion toward the brand.

FBU1: "I used to love going to Le Nordik, especially in the winter. I went about 2 times per month. It was a magical place of peace, tranquility, and rejuvenation. Sadly, it is no longer any of those qualities. While it is fantastic for the company (and the Ottawa- Gatineau region) that it has become such a popular place (and even tourist attraction to the region), it is simply getting too large for its own good. The last time I went (and it wasn't even on a weekend or special holiday), there were just far too many people allowed in at once. It felt more like a penguin colony in a BBC documentary than a place to relax and unwind. Unless Le Nordik starts imposing some kind of entrance quota restrictions (or starts taking reservations to enjoy the spa), I'm afraid Le

Nordik will become more of a public pool than its original roots as a true nature spa."

FBU2: *"totally agree with you!"*

4.2.3 WINTER AT THERMEA

This video was posted on the Thermëa - Winnipeg Facebook page initially on the 13 February 2015 with the title "Discover Winnipeg's newest spa, Thermëa. www.thermea.ca".

It was then published again in the same Facebook page on the 13 January 2016 "Thermëa during winter: a magical experience!", 16 December 2017 "Ferric. Magic. Thermëa" and finally on 16 January 2018 "Winter at Thermëa" with a caption attached saying "The third Monday of January is known as the most depressing day of the year. That's why we've decided to boost your morale with this video containing only the purest spa wellness. The day is looking better already".

The total of comments are 298 comments, the majority of them (250 comments) during 2015, with 1997 likes, 45 loves, 3 wow, which makes deduce an overall positive opinion about the ad.

As said before, the author has decided to analyse all comments from 2015 until 2019, both in English and French, highlighting the following emerged themes.

As in the previous videos, also in this case the users expressed their impatience for their upcoming visit at the spa

"Wow that looks so nice! Can't wait to go"

And

"Can't wait!!!"

Or

"I'm going there tonight can't wait"

Especially for their first visit

"We're heading there tomorrow with my wife, looking forward to our first visit!"

Or for their date with the partners

"I am so looking forward to going I got a day pass and an hour massage for valentine's day"

Another time, people like so much the place shown in the video that they are looking forward to go there

"I wanna go too! Looks fabulous!"

And

"I would love to go ☺"

Or

"I'd like try this. :)"

And

"Oh i want to go"

Or

"It looks so good! I'm definitely going there with my friends ☺ (...)" Sometimes expressing their appreciation writing in capital case "Oh my God"

"OMG can I go there please???"

And

"OMG this is nice i Want To go there (...)"

Or

"OMG sign me up!!!"

Other users instead, despite not living in the area anymore and having waited for the opening, share their intention to go there anyway, given the beauty of the place

"I have been waiting for this place to open for three years, now I don't live there!!!!! I am so making reservations for when I am in Winnipeg next!!!!! This place is remarkable, heading south on Pembina turn left down Chevrier it is just in front of Crescent Golf Course."

Again people are missing the place because of the good experience had

"I want to go back again, and again, and again... Such a wonderful experience!"

Sharing memories about experience that reminds of the world of magic and dreams

"Ça C'était magique! / It was magic!"

"I still dream about it lol"

Others explaining their experience with richness of details, manifesting their joy and happiness

"Whole experience was amazing... indulged in Aufguss twice, so beautiful. Setting changed throughout the day - mist and fog swirled around at times blurring out the sun dancing on the snow

and ice, and blue shadows growing until the magic of sunset. Enjoyed the meals and massage - staff was exceptional, so kind and helpful, very positive. LOVED it!"

Or

"G., my daughter & niece took me there for my birthday. Great experience!!"

Inviting other people to try that experience

"I've been lucky enough to visit the spa twice now. I love it. Absolutely amazing facility. I was blessed with two, not one but two double passes for Christmas this year. I'm a lucky Gal! I'd love to be able to go each month, I'd take my hard working bestie girl friend with me. My husband won't sit still long enough to go but I know DN would be up for it for sure. Happy Anniversary Thermëa!! Many more to come!"

"B. and I spent Friday at Thermea! It was a perfect day! An incredible experience! Everyone should try it!!!"

And

"Its amazing! Go asap! :)"

Or highlighting the feeling of relaxation felt

"Nice place relax your mind loved it thank you (...)"

And

"Just went Saturday night with A. and A. It was so relaxing."

Also in this case, the emotional video gives rise to an appreciation by the users towards the location and the site

"A little bit of Heaven..."

Or

"Oh this looks amazing"

And

"Amazing!"

Or

"It's a beautiful place!"

And

"Sounds awesome"

Or

"Looks like the perfect date"

Or suggesting the visit to other users

"This is a must treat located at 775 Crescent Drive Wpg (Winnipeg)"

Other users explaining and sharing their good experience to friends, paying tribute to the video, suggesting them to go

FBU1: *"FBU2 have you been before?"*

FBU2: *"No...i'm soooo excited. Have you FBU3?"*

FBU3: *"Yes! It is aaaahhhhmazing! S. and I go every year; . In fact we will be there in a few days....our third year. The video is a great overview. Day or night it is time well spent to just 'be'. Enjoy!!!"*

FBU2 "Well you guys enjoy your day there! I've heard nothing but awesome comments about it. Cant wait."

FBU3: "You will love it! You enjoy your day with C.!"

It is important to note that even for this video there was appreciation, in particular users liked this so much as to want to ask, for this reason, information about it and about the music used, with the company itself answering their question

"Very lovely Music"

Or

"Nice place, who is the singer?"

Thermëa - Winnipeg: "You are mine from Holley Maher :)"

And

"Who is the artist that sings during the commercial? Thanks"

Thermëa - Winnipeg: "You are mine from Holley Maher!"

"Thank you! great choice"

Sometimes underlining they cannot wait to go or go back, because of the video itself

"What is the name of the song that they used??"

Thermëa - Winnipeg: "You are mine from Holley Maher :)"

"LOVE IT!! And can't wait to try Thermea!!"

And

"This video makes me want to go back so bad!!"

Others expressed in details what they liked about the ad, starting a conversation and engaging with the company

"I like how a lot of this is filmed in slomo (slow motion). It gives an illusion of relaxation and enjoyment. As opposed to Benny hill like speed (...)"

Thermëa - Winnipeg: "Thank you! It's not an illusion... Thermëa is all about relaxation & enjoyment ;)"

"I'm sure it is, I'm just commenting on the quality of the commercial :)"

Thermëa - Winnipeg: "Yes, thank you :)"

Or referring to other liked emotional video ad, from the same company

"Love the music from this and the summer video as well!"

Once again a feeling of pride emerges, which is translated into tourist advice tips to friends to visit the one that is felt and considered as their own spa, who seem to appreciate the place

FBU1: "FBU2 us Winnipeggers know how to handle the cold, check out our "Nordic Spa" another reason to make the drive up north to visit your cross border friends"

FBU2 "That's fabulous! I wish we had that here!"

Unlikely the other cases, in this one some user manifest their dislike toward the video ad

"Why tease us."

Or

"Too depressing."

Or their aversion toward the brand, whose position is seen as controversial and not comparable to their mission

"Unfortunately, many people in the neighbourhood felt that this spa was foisted upon them, the process for placing this business in a residential neighbourhood was not transparent, the foot print changed after it was approved, there was a lack of consideration for wildlife in the area, and the ongoing fire pit along with the lighting has become a problem for those in the immediate area.".

4.2.4 KALLA TREATMENT

This video was posted on the Nordik Spa-Nature / Chelsea Facebook page initially on the 15 January 2019 with a bilingual title and caption, French and English, saying: "Traitement Källa / Källa treatment. Oubliez la fatigue et le stress. Laissez-vous flotter dans le bassin Källa, un traitement qui vous donnera l'effet d'une bonne nuit de sommeil. / Let stress and tiredness melt away. Experience weightlessness with the Källa treatment. It'll feel like a good night's sleep".

The total of comments are 152 comments, with 124 likes, 43 loves, 5 wow, which makes deduce an overall positive opinion about the ad.

As said before, the author has decided to analyse all comments from 2015 until 2019, both in English and French, highlighting the following emerged themes.

Here as well, users want to let others know their impatience for their upcoming visit trying the treatment at the spa

"J'ai hâte à Samedi / I can not wait for Saturday"

Or

FBU1: "FBU2 can't wait" FBU2: "Omg yas one week"

Or their desire to go and try the treatment experience

"J'ai tellement hâte de déménager là bas pour y aller aussi souvent que je veux! / I can not wait to move there to go as often as I want! ^_^"

And

"Je veux aller la svp (s'il vous plaît)"

Or

"Je veux faire ça / I want to do that"

And

"Would love to experience this 1"

Or

FBU1: "FBU2 faudrait que je t'enmène là / I should take you there"

FBU2: "FBU1 je suis prête quand tu veux. / I'm ready whenever you want."

Some highlighting the feeling of wellbeing and relaxation emerging from the video

FBU1: "FBU2 faudrait l'essayer / should try it. Ça ferait du bien / It would be good 30w"

FBU2: "FBU1 oh que ouui / oh yess"

FBU1: "FBU2 Ok je veux aller la! / Ok I want to go there!"

FBU2: "FBU2 wow ça dont bien l'air cool !! / wow that looks cool !!"

FBU1: "Ca l'air ultra relaxantttt / It looks ultra relaxing"

Planning already a day with friends

FBU1: "FBU2 this looks sooo relaxing"

FBU2: "FBU1 urghhh. Yes. It opened after I was last there and I've been wanting to do it."

FBU1: "Me too!!! We need to find a day and book it off to go. Do we want to do a winter one?"

FBU2: "FBU1 ooohhhh. A week day!"

And

FBU1: "FBU2 FBU3 j'attend toujours on y va quand ? / I'm still waiting when are we going? ;)"

FBU2: "FBU1 omg faut planné ça la / omg must have planned this"

FBU3: "Demain / Tomorrow"

Furthermore, users are again expressing their missing toward the place and willingness to return due to the well-being felt

FBU1: "FBU2 lets go again"

FBU2: "FBU1 omg YES I have never been that relaxed in my whole life love that place"

And

FBU1: "FBU2 ça me manque lol / I miss it lol"

FBU2: "oooo oui!! Gâte-toi ça FBU1, tu le mérite bien! / Treat yourself FBU1, you deserve it!"

Finally, as in the previous cases, the users have manifested their appreciation toward the place and the ad

"The best place"

And

"Un must au Nordik!!"

Or

"Sooo relaxing lololol"

And

"This is amazing!"

Or describing with their initial uncomfortable sensation and the final total relaxation

"The first time I did this it was so creepy. It was like walking down into a flooded dimly lit parking garage and there were bodies floating around. Took a few minutes to get comfortable with that. Water is so salty that you have to lie down; it won't even let you sit up. It's a riot. Felt wonderful. The initial creepiness factor wears off after you relax in the water with ear protection on."

4.3 DISCUSSION

In the following table we can identify and compare the key findings across the four emotional video advertisements, that have been treated independently.

Bearing in mind that the primary aim of this study is to bring to academia and expand the body of knowledge on expressing emotions through the use of social media, in the wellness and spa sector, from the perspective of the brand, and investigate whether emotional marketing can be put in place with the use of social media, influencing the consumer behaviour and understanding their response, the line of inquiry for each case study was focused on:

• Can brands transmit emotions and convey them correctly through the use of social media?
• Which is their impact on consumers?
• Are social media involving consumers' senses influencing their choice and behaviour?

WINTER AT NORDIK	• Impatience; • Desire / Wish; • Nostalgia; • Good Memories; • Appreciation Toward the Place; • Appreciation Toward the Ad; • Pride & Tourism.
MASSANA NATURE IN THE WINTER	• Impatience; • Desire / Wish; • Nostalgia; • Good Memories; • Appreciation Toward the Place; • Appreciation Toward the Ad; • Aversion Toward the Place.

WINTER AT THERMEA	• Impatience; • Desire / Wish; • Nostalgia; • Good Memories; • Appreciation Toward the Place; • Appreciation Toward the Ad; • Pride & Tourism; • Aversion Toward the Ad; • Aversion Toward the Brand.
KALLA TREATMENT	• Impatience; • Desire / Wish; • Nostalgia; • Appreciation Toward the Place; • Appreciation Toward the Ad.

Tab. 3: Emerged Themes

The analysis has shown that emotional marketing, through the use of social media, can influence consumer behaviour since the four videos revealed theirselves as an efficient and successful marketing strategy. Indeed, in each of the four videos, users have perceived them clearly as emotional advertisements, expressing both their appreciation toward the ads, the brand and the places, manifested through their impatience or desire to visit or experience a day at the spa. The vision of the emotional advertisement has stimulated an interest in them, manifesting their nostalgia or willingness to return, because of the very good experiences felt, suggesting to open a new ones closer to them, in order to have the chance to enjoy more experiences, or inviting other people to try that experience. This emerged themes can be recognised as the main one, common to all videos.

Taking into account the case of "Winter at Nordik" and "Winter at Thermae", another important theme that emerged from the analysis is national pride and pride towards a brand belonging to its own territory. This pride is sometimes associated with tourism, translated into recommendations and touristic advice tips, as the place is seen as a touristic attraction or a landmark of the territory, also from people from different areas.

Viewers are not bored by watching emotional advertisements but instead they get positive feelings, encouraging them to live the same experiences and feelings lived by users who, after watching the video, recalled and shared them with other users, suggesting them to live the same beautiful experience.

In fact, as observed by Pine and Gilmore (1999), customers are nowadays looking for new and memorable experiences since good experiences must be memorable, competitive, and produce emotions (Lo, Wu & Tsai, 2015; Pine & Gilmore, 1999), which are the heart of consumer experience (Carù and Cova, 2003). Indeed, organisations must provide customers of satisfactory experiences (Lo & Wu, 2014; Jang & Namkung, 2009; Berry et al., 2002; Babin et al., 1998) since, as found out by Hemmington (2007 quoted in Bharwani and Jahari, 2013) customers buying experiences and memories expect to spend time enjoying a series of memorable personal events, staged by a company (Buxton, 2018), to engage in an inherently personal way (Pine & Gilmore, 1999). Indeed, an experience, occurs when services are purposely used for the involvement of individuals (Pine & Gilmore, 1999). And this can be seen in particular, in the case of Kalla Treatments, where some have highlighted the feeling of wellbeing and total relaxation emerging from the video.

As a matter of fact, the discourse analysis has detected the main reason behind the appreciation of the ad and the brand is a feeling of involvement and engagement, confirming that if videos do not provide emotions, users are not engaged with them, which is a feeling common in all the four cases.

In fact, in the consumption process the element that is most important is precisely emotions (Lo & Wu, 2014; Jang & Namkung, 2009; Babin et al., 1998) as in response to a service, the individual has the so-called "emotion of consumption", or an emotional reaction without which the service is no longer satisfactory (Lo, Wu, Tsai, 2015; Richins, 1997).

This feeling of engagement is also expressed by users sharing their positive experiences at the spa shown in the videos, and this involvement leads to a clear stated desire of going in the advertised place, which is an index of success of the emotional marketing video. Indeed, wellness and spa companies should use social media to create profitable interactions with customers. Those interactions could create competitive advantage over their services as, the value determined by this interaction, can help develop propositions of value more oriented to their customer's desires (Lagrosen & Grundén, 2014).

It is also of considerable importance to put focus on some comments regarding the video itself, in particular in the case of "Winter at Nordik" and "Winter at Thermae" that highlighted the power of relaxation emerging from the video, paying tribute to it or asking information about it, with the company itself answering to them, which led to the start of a conversation and engagement between the user and the company.
Or, in the case of "Massana Nature", users shared all the details of their stay, recommending the spa to other viewers, and the Group Nordik responded to thank them and inviting them for other visits. All these can be seen as a successful engagement with digital users.

Confirming previous research (Lagrosen & Grundén, 2014), findings have shown and highlighted the value of interaction on social media, in order to create meaningful relationships with customers. The interaction on social media is created by active contributions from consumers and producers, in which the customer is always a precious co-producer (Lagrosen & Grundén, 2014). Spas have a vast knowledge on how to create pleasant and healthy experiences, being the basis of their services, and sharing them on social media should be on a large scale (Lagrosen & Grundén, 2014).
Indeed, it is of considerable importance some comments regarding the video itself, that highlighted the power of relaxation emerging from the video, pay tribute to it or asking information about it, with the company itself answering which led to the start of a conversation and engagement between the user and the company.

However, a deeper examination reveals that other viewers took a completely different position which is categorised in an aversion toward the ads and the brands, in particular in the case of "Massana Nature" and "Winter at Thermea".

For some users watching the video reminds of bad experiences at the spa, which is translated in putting it in a bad light. The motivations of negative evaluations is because the brand position is seen as controversial and and no longer comparable to their mission.

5 CONCLUSIONS AND RECOMMENDATIONS

In conclusion, the critical review of the literature regarding the use of social media marketing, within the spa and wellness industry, as a way of expressing and convey emotions to customers, has highlighted some gaps in the industry.

Indeed, the spa and wellness industry is increasingly expanding in most of the world (Lagrosen & Grundén, 2014), but despite that (Buxton, 2018; Global Wellness Institute, 2014; Tabacchi, 2010), there is still very little research done in this area, almost neglected by researchers, and largely unexplored (Lagrosen & Grundén, 2014). Several authors have requested further studies (Guillet & Kucukusta, 2016; Buxton, 2018; Loureiro et al., 2013; Reitsamer, 2015) as an opportunity to investigate factors that contribute to the formation of memorable experiences (Pine & Gilmore, 1998) and many have written about how to involve the customer in order to get this experience, with managers offering unique and multi-sensory experiences to create value (Berry et al., 2002).

Recent studies have shown how purchasing choices and decisions are the result of a careful analysis of rational and emotional aspects, since emotions play a key role in any kind of social or business decision (Cislaghi, 2011). A good marketing strategy identifies how to give the opportunity to live a memorable experience (Ferrari, 2016, 2009, 2005; Pine & Gilmore, 1999). These results are of obvious importance for marketing and communication studies as it can be an effective means of pushing to buy, implemented by strong brands by exploiting their benefits in terms of performance, to achieve an emotional agreement with consumers (Ferrari, 2016).

The relationship between companies and their audiences has been changed by the arrival of the web, digital media and technological interfaces, which give the opportunity to affirm their long-neglected needs, relying on entrepreneurial choices and strategies, as well as interpreting needs. People can not only guide the choices of brands and companies but also participate actively (Maestri & Sassoon, 2017).

Given the rapid development of social media and web 2.0, changing people's habits and the conditions for marketing (Lagrosen & Grundén, 2014; Ruane & Wallace, 2013) wellness and spa companies should use social media to create profitable interactions with customers. Those interactions could create competitive advantage over their services as, the value determined by this interaction, can help develop propositions of value more oriented to their customer's desires (Lagrosen & Grundén, 2014). In fact, previous research has highlighted the value of interaction on social media, in order to create meaningful relationships with customers. Spas have a vast knowledge on how to create pleasant and healthy experiences, being the basis of their services, and sharing them on social media should be on a large scale (Lagrosen & Grundén, 2014).

For this reason, the aim of this study is to bring to academia and investigate whether emotional marketing through the use of social media can influence consumer behaviour, in the wellness and spa sector. This, evaluating the efficacy of the Canadian Groupe Nordik's communication strategy, analysing comments of four emotional advertisement videos posted on the Facebook accounts of the company.

In doing so, the research questions that have been set for this analysis are:
• Can brands transmit emotions and convey them correctly through the use of social
   media?
• Which is their impact on consumers?

5 CONCLUSION AND RECOMMENDATIONS

• Are social media involving consumers' senses influencing their choice and behaviour?

The author has decided to choose a qualitative oriented study with an inductive approach in the form of a case study. A discourse analysis of the comments has been deployed of four videos which were chosen following certain criteria such as the emotional impact given, the relevance to the study, the high number of comments, views and likes, representing discussion and debate, in addition to the discreet richness of discourse (Calder, 1977). The research method deployed is Netnography, or Internet ethnography, an online qualitative marketing research, adapted to the study of online communities of consumers (Kozinets, 2002). The videos were analysed individually, using the analytical structure and the key lines that emerged from the literature. The key results were then recombined and the common themes identified and discussed, reflecting on those specific to each one.

The analysis has shown that emotional marketing, through the use of social media, can influence consumer behaviour since the four videos revealed theirselves as an efficient and successful marketing strategy: consumers expressed both their appreciation toward the ads, the brand and the places, manifesting their impatience to visit and experience a day at the spa, as the vision of the emotional ad has stimulated an interest in them, or their desire to return due to their good memories of the good experience had at the place. This can be seen as the main emerged themes common to all videos. Moreover, viewers are not bored by watching emotional advertisements, as happens with the usual commercials, and the main reason for that, detected by the discourse analysis, is a feeling of involvement and engagement, confirming that if videos do not provide emotions, users are not engaged with them. This feeling of engagement is also expressed by users sharing their positive experiences at the spa shown in the videos, and this involvement leads to a clear stated desire of going in the advertised place, which is an index of success of the emotional marketing video. Indeed, wellness and spa companies should use social media to create profitable interactions with customers.

Those interactions could create competitive advantage over their services as, the value determined by this interaction, can help develop propositions of value more oriented to their customer's desires (Lagrosen & Grundén, 2014).

Another important theme that emerged from the analysis is national pride and pride towards a brand belonging to its own territory. This pride is sometimes associated with tourism, translated into recommendations and touristic advice tips, as the place is seen as a touristic attraction or a landmark of the territory, also from people from different areas.

Confirming previous research (Lagrosen & Grundén, 2014), findings have also shown and highlighted the value of interaction on social media, in order to create meaningful relationships with customers. However, other viewers expressed their aversion toward the ads and the brands, whose motivations is the brand position seen as controversial and no longer comparable to their mission.

This study wants to bring to academia and expand the body of knowledge on expressing emotions through the use of social media, influencing consumer behaviour, in the wellness and spa sector, from the perspective of the brand.

This research has several limitations: first of all, it was carried out only in one sector, in one country and with only one case study and for this reason, there are uncertain possibilities of generalising the results to other contexts; furthermore, the study was based on qualitative methodology and quantitative research, with results related to this study, would be interesting for future research.

BIBLIOGRAPHY

Alharbi, A. (2015). *Business growth through social media marketing.* International Journal of Innovation and Applied Studies. Vol. 13, ISS. 4 Available at: http:// www.ijias.issr-journals.org/ [Accessed 7 January 2019].

Babin, B. J., Darden, W. R., & Babin, L. A. (1998). *Negative emotions in marketing research: Affect or artifact?.* Journal of Business Research, 42(3), pp. 271–285.

Backstrom, L. (2013). *News Feed FYI: A window into News Feed.* Retrieved from https://www.facebook.com/business/news/News-Feed-FYI-A-Window-Into-News-Feed.

Barrett, L. F. (2009). *Variety is the spice of life: A psychological construction approach to understanding variability in emotion.* Cognition and Emotion, 23(7), 1284-1306.

Bharwani, S., & Jahari, V. (2013). *An exploratory study of competencies required to co- create memorable customer experiences in the hospitality industry.* International Journal of Contemporary Hospitality Management, 25(6), 823–863.

Boccia Artieri, G. (2004) *I media-mondo. Forme e linguaggi dell'esperienza contemporanea.* Roma: Meltemi.

Bærenholdt, J. O. & Sundbo, J. (eds) (2007). *Oplevelsesøkonomi: Produktion, forbrug, kultur.* København: Samfundslitteratur.

Bensky, T., & Fisher, E. (2014). *Internet and emotions.* New York: Routledge.

Berry, L. L., Carbone, L. P. and Haeckel, S. H. (2002). *Managing the Total Customer Experience.* Available at: https://sloanreview.mit.edu/article/managing-the-total- customer-experience/ [Accessed on 1 June 2019].

Boyd, D. M., & Ellison, N. B. (2007). *Social network sites: Definition, history, and scholarship.* Journal of Computer-Mediated Communication, 13(1), 210-230.

Bruckman, A. (2006). *Teaching Students to Study Online Communities Ethically.* Journal of Information Ethics, 15(2), 82–98. doi: 10.3172/jie.15.2.82

Bryman, A. (2015). *Social Research Methods,* Oxford, Oxford University Press.

Bryman, A., Lewis-Beck, M.S. & Liao, T.F. (2004). The Sage encyclopedia of social science research methods, Thousand Oaks: Sage.

Burrell, G. and Morgan, G. (1979) *Sociological Paradigms and Organisational Analysis.* London: Heinemann.

Buttle, F. (1998) *Word of mouth: understanding and managing referral marketing.* Journal of Strategic Marketing, 6(3), 241-254.

Buxton, L. (2018) *Destination spas and the creation of memorable guest experiences*, International Journal of Spa and Wellness, 1:2, 133-138, Available at: DOI: 10.1080/24721735.2018.1493778 [Accessed on 1 June 2019].

Caffier, E. (2017) *The Social Spa Concept Design. An investigation of innovative experience services which need to be included in a spa concept to encourage socializing. A case study of*

Germany. (Master Thesis).

Calder, B. (1977). *"Focus Groups and the Nature of Qualitative Research,"* Journal of Marketing Research, 14 (3), 353–64.

Carù, A., & Cova, B. (2003). *Revisiting consumption experience: A more humble but complete view of the concept.* Marketing Theory, 3(2), 267–286.

Cavanagh S. (1997) *Content analysis: concepts, methods and applications.* Nurse Researcher 4, 5– 16.

Charlesworth, A. (2009) *Internet marketing.* Oxford: Elsevier.

Chaffey, D., Ellis-Chadwick, F. (2016) *Digital Marketing: Strategy, implementation and practice.* UK: Pearson.

Chaffey, D., Ellis-Chadwick, F. (2019) *Digital Marketing: Strategy, implementation and practice.* UK: Pearson.

Chaffey, D., Smith, P. R., & Smith, P. R. (2017). *Digital marketing excellence: planning and optimizing your online marketing.* New York: Routledge.

Cislaghi, A. (2011) *Il marketing sensoriale e il suo impatto sul consumatore nel settore del lusso.* Bachelor's Thesis.

Cole, F.L. (1988) *Content analysis: process and application.* Clinical Nurse Specialist 2(1), 53–57.

Corbin, C. B., & Pangrazi, R. P. (2001). *Toward a uniform definition of wellness: A commentary present's council on physical fitness and sports.* Research Digest, 3(15), 1– 8.

Corbin, J., Strauss, A. (2008). *Basics of Qualitative Research*, London, SAGE.

Crotty, M. (1998) *The Foundations of Social Research.* London: Sage.

Denzin, N.K. and Lincoln, Y.S. (2011) *'Introduction: The discipline and practice of qualitative research',* in N.K. Denzin and Y.S. Lincoln (eds) The Sage Handbook of Qualitative Research (4th edn). London: Sage, pp. 1–19.

Denzin N., Lincoln. Y., (2013). *Collecting and interpreting qualitative materials,* Thousand Oaks, SAGE

Denzin, N., Lincoln, Y., (2013). *The landscape of qualitative research,* Los Angeles, SAGE.

Eisenhardt, K.M. (1989) *'Building theories from case study research',* Academy of Management Review, Vol. 14, No. 4, pp. 532–50.

Dyer, W. G., Jr, Wilkins, A. L., & Eisenhardt, K. M. (1991). *Better stories, not better constructs, to generate better theory: A rejoinder to Eisenhardt; better stories and better constructs: The case for rigor and comparative logic.* The Academy of Management Review, 16(3), 613.

Eisenhardt, K.M. and Graebner, M.E. (2007) *'Theory building from cases: Opportunities and challenges',* Academy of Management Journal, Vol. 50, No. 1, pp. 25–32.

Ekman, P. (1992). *An argument for basic emotions.* Cognition and Emotion, 6(3-4), 169-200.

Ekman, P. (1999). *Basic emotions.* In T. Dalgleish & M. Power (Eds.), Handbook of Cognition and Emotion (pp. 45-60). Sussex, U.K.: John Wiley & Sons

Elo, S., Kyngas, H. (2008) *The qualitative content analysis process.* Journal of Advanced Nursing 62(1), 107–115.

Ely, J. (2008). *Cultivating customer loyalty: The secret is in *the service.* Spa Management, 18(5), 56–60.

Evans, D., Bratton, S. (2008) *Social media marketing.* Indianapolis: Wiley.

Fairclough, N. (1995). *Language and power.* London: Longman.

Fairclough, N. (1989). *Michel Foucault and the analysis of discourse.* Lancaster: Centre for Language in Social Life, Lancaster University.

Ferrari, T. (2005) *Comunicare l'impresa. Realtà e trend polisensoriale-emozionale.* Editore: CLUEB. 1st Edition.

Ferrari, T. (2016) *Comunicare l'impresa. Realtà e trend polisensoriale-emozionale.* Editore: CLUEB. 2nd Edition.

Ferrari, T. (2009) *Marketing e Comunicazione Non Convenzionale. Guerrilla, Virale, Polisnesoriale, Emozionale.* Editore: CLUEB.

Ferraresi, M, Schmitt, B, H. (2018). *Marketing Esperienziali: Come Sviluppare l'esperienza di consumo.* Italy: FrancoAngeli.

Flick, U. (2014) *The Sage Handbook of Qualitative Data Analysis.* London: SAGE Publications.

Fredrickson, B. L. (2001). *The role of positive emotion in positive psychology: the broaden-and- build theory of positive emotion.* American Psychologist, 56(3), 218-226. Gallucci, F. (2014) Marketing Emozionale e Neuroscienze. Italy: Egea.

Global Wellness Institute. (2014). *Global spa & wellness economy monitor.* New York: Global Wellness Institute.

Gobe', M. (2003) *Emotional identity.* Global Cosmetic Industry [Accessed 7 January 2019]. Available at: http://www.proquest.com/

Golbeck, J. (2015). *Introduction to social media investigation: a hands-on approach.* Waltham, MA: Syngress.

Gretzel, U., Yoo, K. H., (2008) *Use and impact of online travel reviews.* Information and Communication Technologies in Tourism, 2, 35-46.

Groupe Nordik (2019) *Who We Are.* Available at: https://www.groupenordik.com/en/ about-us/who-we-are/ [Accessed on 1 June 2019]

Gubrium, J. F. and Holstein, J. A. (2014) *Analytic Inspiration in Ethnographic Fieldwork.* In Flick, U. (2014) The Sage Handbook of Qualitative Data Analysis. London: SAGE Publications

Guillet, D., & Kucukusta, D. B. (2016). *Measuring spa-goers' preferences: A conjoint analysis approach.* International Journal of Hospitality Management, 45, 115–124.

Gustafsson, J. (2017) *Single case studies vs. multiple case studies: A comparative study.* Available at: https://pdfs.semanticscholar.org/ae1f/ 06652379a8cd56654096815dae801a59cba3.pdf [Accessed on 1 June 2019]

Hall, S. (Ed.). (1997). *Culture, media and identities. Representation: Cultural representations and signifying practices.* Thousand Oaks, CA, US: Sage Publications, Inc; Maidenhead, BRK, England: Open University Press.

Hansson, L., Wrangmo, A. and Solberg Soilen, K. (2013), "Optimal ways for companies to use Facebook as a marketing channel", Journal of Information, Communication and Ethics in Society, Vol. 11 No. 2, pp. 112-126.

Holbrook, M. B. (1999). *Consumer value: A framework for analysis and research.* London, England; New York, NY: Routledge.

Holbrook, M. B., & Hirschman, E. C. (1982). *The experiential aspects of consumption: Consumer fantasies, feelings and fun.* Journal of Consumer Research, 9(2), 132–140.

Jang, S., & Namkung, Y. (2009). *Perceived quality, emotions, and behavioral intentions: Application of an extended Mehrabian–Russell model to restaurants.* Journal of Business Research, 62(4), pp.451–460. doi:10.1016/j.jbusres.2008.01.038.

Johnstone, B. (2018) *Discourse Analysis.* UK: Wiley Blackwell.

Kapadia A. (2016) *Numbers Don't Lie: What a 2016 Nielsen Study Revealed About Referrals.* Available at: https://www.business2community.com/marketing/numbers-dont- lie-2016-nielsen-study-revealed-referrals-01477256 Accessed on: [7 January 2019].

Kappas, A., & Krämer, N. C. (2011). *Face-to-face communication over the Internet: emotions in a web of culture, language, and technology.* Cambridge, UK: Cambridge University Press.

Karatzogianni, A. and Kuntsman, A. (Eds). (2012) *Digital Cultures and the Politics of Emotion. Language and Dialogue*, 3(3), 482–484. doi: 10.1075/ld.3.3.09fel

Kynga¨s H. & Vanhanen L. (1999) *Content analysis* (Finnish). Hoitotiede 11, 3–12. Kotler, P., Bowen, J. T., Makens, J. C., Baloglu, S. B. (2018) Marketing del Turismo: Settima Edizione. Italy: Pearson.

Kotler, P., Keller, K., Ancarani, F. (2017) *Marketing Management.* Quattordicesima Edizione. Italy: Pearson.

Kozinets, R. V.; Dolbec, P. Earley, A. (2014) *Netnographic*

Analysis: Understanding Culture through Social Media Data. In Flick, U. (2014) The Sage Handbook of Qualitative Data Analysis. London: SAGE Publications.

Kozinets, R. V. (2010). *Netnography: ethnographic research in the age of the internet.* Thousand Oaks, CA: Sage Publications Ltd.

Kozinets, R. V. (2002) *The Field Behind the Screen: Using Netnography for Marketing Research in Online Communities.* Journal of Marketing Research: February 2002, Vol. 39, No. 1, pp. 61-72.

Langer, R., & Beckman, S. C. (2005). *Sensitive research topics: netnography revisited.* Qualitative Market Research: An International Journal, 8(2), 189–203. doi: 10.1108/13522750510592454

Lagrosen, S. O., Grundén, K., (2014) *"Social media marketing in the wellness industry",* The TQM Journal, Vol. 26 Issue: 3, pp.253-260, Available at: https://doi.org/ 10.1108/TQM-12-2013-0129 [Accessed on: 1 June 2019].

Lagrosen, S. and Josefsson, P. (2011), *"Social media marketing as an entrepreneurial learning process",* International Journal of Technology Marketing, Vol. 6 No. 4, pp. 331-340.

Larivie`re, B., Joosten, H., Malthouse, E.C., van Birgelen, M., Aksoy, P., Kunz, W.H. and Huang, M.-H. (2013), *"Value fusion – the blending of consumer and firm value in the distinct context of mobile technologies and social media",* Journal of Service Management, Vol. 24 No. 3, pp. 268-293.

LeDoux, J. E. (2014). *Comment: What's basic about the brain mechanisms of emotion? Emotion Review,* 6(4), 318-320.

Leung, D., Law, R., Van Hoof, H., Buhalis, D., (2013) *Social media in tourism and hospitality: a literature review.* Journal of Travel Tour Mark, 30 (1-2), 3-22.

Lo, A. S. & Wu, C., (2014). *Effect of Consumption Emotion on Hotel and Resort Spa Experience.* Journal of Travel & Tourism Marketing, 31(8), pp. 958–984.

Lo, A., Wu, C. & Tsai, H., (2015). *The Impact of Service Quality on Positive Consumption Emotions in Resort and Hotel Spa Experiences.* Journal of Hospitality Marketing & Management, 24(2), pp.155–179.

Loureiro, S. M. C., Almieda, M., & Rita, P. (2013). *The effect of atmospheric cues and involvement on pleasure and relaxation: The spa hotel context.* International Journal of Hospitality Management, 35, 35–43.

Maestri, A., Sassoon, J. (2017) *Customer Experience Design: Progettare esperienze di marca memorabili sui media digitali.* Italy: FrancoAngeli.

McNeil, K. R., & Ragins, E. J. (2005). *Staying in the spa marketing game: Trends, challenges, strategies and techniques.* Journal of Vacation Marketing, 11(1) 31–39.

Mertens, D. M. (2014). *Mixed Methods and Wicked Problems.* Journal of Mixed Methods Research, 9(1), 3–6. doi: 10.1177/1558689814562944

Minichiello, V., Aroni, R., Timewell, E. and Alexander, L. (1990). *In-Depth Interviewing: Researching People.* Hong Kong: Longman Cheshire.

Monteson, P. A., & Singer, J. (2004). *Marketing a resort-based spa.* Journal of Vacation Marketing, 10(3), 282–290.

Nilsen, B. T., (2015) *The Production and Consumption of Experiences: A Study of the Spa Industry in Norway,* PhD Degree Thesis, Norwegian University of Science and Technology, Faculty of Social Sciences and Technology, Management Department of Geography.

Panger, G. T. (2017) *Emotion in Social Media*. Ph.D. dissertation. University of California, Berkeley.

Parker, I. (1992). *Discourse dynamics: Critical analysis for social and individual psychology.* Florence, KY, US: Taylor & Frances/Routledge.

Perini, R. (2010) *Marketing Emozionale (Emotional Marketing)* Available at: http:// www.riccardoperini.com/marketing-emozionale.php [Accessed on: 7 January 2019].

Pine, J., & Gilmore, J. (1999). *The experience economy.* Boston, MA: Harvard Business School Press.

Pine, B. J., & Gilmore, J. H. (2011). *The experience economy.* Boston: Harvard Business Review Press.

Pine, B. J., & Gilmore, J. H. (1998). *Welcome to the Experience Economy.* Harvard Business Review.

Plutchik, R. (1995) *Psicologia e Biologia delle Emozioni.* Italy: Bollati Boringhieri.

Prasad, D. B. (2008) *Content analysis: A method of Social Science Research,* In D.K. Lal Das (ed) Research Methods for Social Work, (pp.174-193), New Delhi: Rawat Publications.

Potter, J. and Hepburn, A., 2005. *Qualitative interviews in psychology: problems and possibilities.* Qualitative Research in Psychology, 2 (4), pp.281-307. Routledge (Taylor & Francis) / Edward Arnold (Publishers) Ltd

Reavey, P. (2011). *Visual methods in psychology: using and interpreting images in qualitative research.* New York: Routledge.

Reitsamer, B. F. (2015). *Post-consumptive experience in ser-*

vicescapes: *The impact of mental reenactment on consumers' loyalty*. AMA winter educators' proceedings, Chicago (pp. 6–14).

Remedios, P. (2008). *Built environment-spa design*. In M. Cohen & G. Bodeker (Eds.), Understanding the global spa industry: Spa management (pp. 281–296). Oxford, England: Butterworth-Heinemann.

Richins, M. L. (1997). *Measuring emotions in the consumption experience*. Journal of Consumer Research, 24(2), pp. 127–146.

Roberts, K. (2005) *Lovemarks*. Il futuro oltre il brand. Milano: Mondadori.

Ruane, L., & Wallace, E. (2013). *Generation Y females online: insights from brand narratives*. Qualitative Market Research: An International Journal, 16(3), 315–335. doi: 10.1108/13522751311326125

Russell, J. A. (2003). *Core affect and the psychological construction of emotion*. Psychological Review, 110(1), 145-172.

Russell, J. A. (2009). *Emotion, core affect, and psychological construction*. Cognition and Emotion, 23(7), 1259-1283.

Sabini, J., & Silver, M. (2005). *Ekman's basic emotions: Why not love and jealousy? Cognition and Emotion*, 19(5), 693-712.

Saunders, M., Lewis, P., Thornhill, A. (2009) *Research methods for business students*. Harlow : Financial Times Prentice Hall.

Saunders, M., Lewis, P., Thornhill, A. (2015) *Research methods for business students*. New York : Pearson Education.

Schmitt, B. H. (1999). *Experiential marketing*. Journal of marketing management, 15(1-3), 53-67. The Free Press, New

York.

Scott, D.M. (2010), *The New Rules of Marketing and PR: How to Use Social Media, Blogs, News Releases,* Online Video and Viral Marketing to Reach Buyers Directly, 2nd ed., John Wiley & Sons, Hoboken, NJ.

Shaw, S. E., & Bailey, J. (2009). *Discourse analysis: what is it and why is it relevant to family practice?.* Family practice, 26(5), 413-9.

Shupletcova, T. (2017) *Emotional Branding in Social Media Case: Barcelona Home*, Bachelor's Thesis.

Smith, M. K., Ferrari, S., Puczkò, L. (2016) *Service Innovations and Experience Creation in Spas,* Wellness and Medical Tourism. In Sotiriadis, M., Gursoy, D. (2016) The Handbook of Managing and Marketing Tourism Experiences.

Smith, M. K., Ferrari, S., Puczkò, L. (2014). *Co-creating Spa Customer Experience.* In Kandampully, J., Customer Experience Management: Enhancing Experience and Value through Service Management. Dubuque, USA: Kendall Hunt, pp. 187-203.

Tabacchi, M. H. (2010). *Current research and events in the spa industry.* Cornell Hospitality Quarterly, 51(1), 102–117.

Tettegah, S. Y. (2016). *Emotions and technology: Communication of feelings for, with, and through digital media. Emotions, technology, and social media.* San Diego, CA, US: Elsevier Academic Press.

Titscher, S., Meyer, M., Wodak, R., Vetter, E. (2000). *Methods of Text and Discourse Analysis: In Search of Meaning.* Sage Publications.

Tracy, J. L. (2014). *An evolutionary approach to understanding distinct emotions. Emotion Review*, 6(4), 308-312.

Tuten, T. L., Solomon, M. R. (2014) *Social Media Marketing: Post-consumo, innovazione collaborativa e valore condiviso.* Italy: Pearson.

Van Dijk, T. A. (1993). *Principles of Critical Discourse Analysis. Discourse & Society*, 4(2), 249–283. doi: 10.1177/0957926593004002006

Veal, A., (2011). *Research methods for leisure and tourism,* Harlow, Financial Times Prentice Hall.

Veal, A., Burton, C., (2014). *Research Methods for arts and event management,* Harlow, Pearson Education Limited.

Westbrook, R. A., & Oliver, R. L. (1991). *The dimensionality of consumption emotion patterns and consumer satisfaction.* Journal of Consumer Research, 18(1), pp. 84–91.

Willig, C. (2014) *Discourses and Discourse Analysis.* In Flick, U. (2014)The Sage Handbook of Qualitative Data Analysis. London: SAGE Publications.

Wittgenstein, L. (1984). *Philosophical investigations.* Oxford: B. Blackwell.

Wodak, R. (1996). *Disorders of discourse.* London: Longman.

Wodak, R. (1989). *Language, Power and Ideology Studies in political discourse.* Amsterdam: John Benjamins Publishing Company.

Wundt, W. (1896) *Introduction to Outlines of Psychology.* In Wozniak, R. H. (1999). Classics in Psychology, 1855-1914: Historical Essays. Bristol, UK: Thoemmes Press.

Wuttke, M., & Cohen, M. (2008). *Spa retail.* In M. Cohen & G. Bodeker (Eds.), Understanding the global spa industry:

Spa management (pp. 208–220). Oxford, England: Butterworth-Heinemann.

Ye, Q., Law, R., Gu, B., Chen, W., (2011) *The influence of user-generated content on traveler behavior: An empirical investigation on the effects of e-word-of-mouth to hotel online bookings.* Computers in Human Behavior, 27(2), 634-639.

Yin, R.K. (2014) *Case Study Research: Design and Method* (5th Edn). London: Sage. Yin, R. K. (2003) Case study research: Design and methods. Thousand Oaks, CA: Sage.

NOTES

NOTES

NOTES

NOTES

NOTES

NOTES

NOTES

www.ingramcontent.com/pod-product-compliance
Lightning Source LLC
Chambersburg PA
CBHW070931160426
43193CB00011B/1659